WOMEN EMPLOYEES AND RURAL DEVELOPMENT
(Problems of Employed Women in Rural Areas)

WOMEN EMPLOYEES AND RURAL DEVELOPMENT

(Problems of Employed Women in Rural Areas)

Dr. ANURADHA BHOITE

Gian Publishing House

29/6 SHAKTI NAGAR • DELHI-110007 • INDIA

GIAN PUBLISHING HOUSE
29/6 Shakti Nagar, Delhi-110007

ISBN 81-212-0085-7

PRINTED IN INDIA

Published by Mrs. Gayatri Garg for Gian Publishing House, Delhi and Printed at Mohan Printing Corpn. Padam Nagar, Delhi-110007.

DEDICATED TO THE MEMORY OF MY LOVING MOTHER WHO WOULD HAVE GIVEN HER PLEASANT SMILE TO SEE THE RESEARCH WORK IN PRINT, BUT ALAS !

PREFACE

AFTER Independence, Government launched community Development Programme for bringing about all round progress of the rural masses. However, in the initial stages no serious attempts were made to cover the welfare of the women under these schemes. But later on it was realized that the success of CDP greatly depended on the co-operation and tacit acceptance of it by the rural women, too. Through this realization, as a part of the development programme, the cadre of women workers was created for bettering the conditions of rural women-folk.

The introduction of these developmental schemes opened up a wide vista of employment opportunities for women. Many needy women, mostly from Urban area, sought these opportunities and took up the jobs as primary and secondary school teachers, Gramsevikas, Nurses, Nurse-midwives, Auxiliary Nurse Midwives, Health visitors, Family Planning Workers and the like.

The overall nature of the role of these women employees was to initiate and assist the process of social change in the form of modernization of rural life. Their task was to act as agents of deliberately introduced change.

But the rural situation was not ripe enough to welcome the change. Things were not working smoothly for these women employees and they were confronted with various problems in the rural setting. To cite one, a number of cases of their harassment in rural areas, were reported in the newspapers and were discussed on the floor of Maharashtra legislature at that time. My concern and inquisitiveness prompted me to undertake the study of their problems for my doctoral degree (1973) in Sociology. Studies of the various facets of Urban Women were undertaken by quite a few sociologists. But the employed women in rural areas were neglected in this respect. So I thought it essential to study their problems. I hope the present inquiry would be of some value to our social policy makers and also for further research. The book is based on my above mentioned doctoral work.

Reader
Department of Sociology
University of Poona
Ganeshkhind, Pune-411007

ANURADHA BHOITE

ACKNOWLEDGEMENTS

Now I consider, it as my primary duty to express my deep sense of gratitude to those without whose co-operation and guidance the research as well as the book would not have seen the light of the day.

First of all I am deeply indebted to my guide Prof. Y.B. Damle, whose constant encouragement and wise counsel were always the valuable props to lean on during the preparation of the work.

I consider it as my duty to acknowledge the debt I owe to Prof. Walunjkar, Prof. Dhanagare, Prof. Mrs. Neeraben Desai, Prof. Mrs. Kaldate and colleagues in the Sociology Department of Marathwada University, my present colleagues in the Department of Sociology of University of Poona and Prof. Hiremath of Sociology Department of Karnataka University, for their uniform helpfulness in this academic endeavour.

I verbalize here my immense thanks to Shri J.L. Guptaji of Gian Publishing House, New Delhi, for readily accepting the manuscript and bringing it in the book from within a short time.

Last but not the least, I owe a large chunk of my gratitude to my husband-colleague, Prof. Uttam Bhoite, who provided the original stimulus to this work and who is always an unfailing source of sound advice and inspiration to me.

Finally I thank my children, Jaideep and Akshara, otherwise they would feel neglected !

ANURADHA BHOITE

LIST OF TABLES

CONTENTS

took up the jobs as primary and secondary school teachers, Gramsevikas of various categories, Nurse-midwives, Auxiliary Nurse-midwives, Health-visitors, Family planning workers etc.

These various developmental schemes can be described sociologically as institutionalised changes introduced in a traditional Society. The change intended in these schemes is in the nature of modernizing peasant society in all possible directions as these schemes were innovative in nature.

An analysis of the roles of these women employees reveals that they have to act as the agents of institutionalised change. The work assigned to these women is to persuade the women folk in the villages to accept the scientific outlook in all the matters of life and to discard the age-old habits and change their outlook which retard the intended progress. This shows that their role is to help the process of modernization through institutionalised change introduced in rural community, provided, modernization means acceptance of means and goals based on rational calculation.

Somehow or the other, innovations always disturb the established patterns of behaviour. So change is often resisted in every society. Much more in a tradition-bound society like India, where old ways of behaviour are regarded as sacrosanct. In such a society, it becomes difficult for an innovator to play his role. Indian village, even today, has retained its traditional outlook inspite of various forces of modernization impinging on it, in modern times. Cormack has succinctly pointed out this aspect of Indian rural community in the following manner. She observes, "The pattern of life in India is based upon the village, and urban life developed from this pattern. It is a safe generalization to say that village life tends to be more conservative with more adherence to traditional patterns."[2]

The traditional values and norms of behaviour even now, govern the attitudes and way of living of a large section of the rural community. Traditional inhibitions and stereotypes are still deeply embedded in the hard core of the ethic of Indian society. Naturally, old values and notions regarding the status and role of woman have not undergone much change. The employment of woman in itself is viewed as an anachronism in the existing traditional structure.

By tradition and custom, the role of woman in the Indian society has been that of daughter, wife and mother. Cormack (1953) study underscores these very roles of women in India. She observes, "They are proud to be women, to be wives, to be mothers. Any new aspect of their role must come second to this primary function."[3] It may be pertinent here to mention the point of view expressed by an Indian informant of Dr. Cormack about the function of Hindu woman. "Cormack described the function of woman as three-fold to be an ideal daughter, an ideal wife, an ideal mother. These three concepts can't be separated. To obey the father, to worship the husband, and to take care of the children, they all go together."[4]

Prabhu's (1963) analysis of the Indian attitude towards women exposes the same point of view. He says, "Women's part was perhaps supposed to be in the conserving and propagation of the race ; and these functions were probably thought to be naturally inherited by her."[5]

Kapadia (1966) contributes to the same view towards woman. He comments, "Educational, economic and political rights having been guaranteed, the social milieu is conducive to the attainment of social equality. At the same time the traditional ideal of Pativrata is strong, and trends are in evidence which work against the implementation of the ideal of Social Justice and indirectly lend support to the traditional values."[6] This shows the persistence of conservatism and traditionalism in India about the role of woman, both in rural as well as in urban sectors.

However, there is no point in denying the fact that in the rural areas, by and large, women do work on farms and help other members of the family in their normal chores. But a close scrutiny reveals, that most of these women work on their own, family farms and co-operative with their own family members in productive activities. The idea of woman working outside the family on wages is not favourably received in India.

A sort of stigma is attached to the woman and her family, if she works outside the home for remuneration, which is seen even in villages. Women belonging to the lowest economic and social strata only, work outside the family orbit in rural areas. The following remark of Gadgil (1965) reflects the general aversion of Indian people, rural as well as urban, towards economic activities of women outside the family. "Non-participation of women in any work and particularly manual work outdoor is everywhere considered as a value."[7]

Employment of women as is understood in the modern sense, is yet to be socially recognized in Indian society. Especially, the rural people are not at all accustomed to this role of woman. The cadre of women employees in the rural sector is created only after the Independence. So it is not at all surprising that the domestic setting, as the accepted framework of woman's life and work still underlies the pattern of women's expected role, in rural India.

In such circumstances the employed woman is bound to suffer from various kinds of difficulties resulting from conflicting demands put on her. She is likely to be torn between the two pressures working on her simultaneously, one to be a good housewife and another to be an efficient employee. Torn between these two incompatible loyalties, she is bound to suffer. In such a case the very purpose of employing her is likely to be defeated.

Lately, some of her problems have caught the attention of the people. Harassment of women employees in villages has been the topic of serious public discussion in recent times. A number of cases of harassment of women employees were reported in the newspapers and the same were discussed vehemently on the floor of Maharashtra Legislature. Such public issues are always discussed on the level of personal opinions and emotions rather than on the basis of rational analysis of Sociological facts. Such facts are, however, essential for a proper assessment of the situation and a sober evaluation of the different sides of the problem. This study of the problems of employed women in rural community was undertaken with this consideration in mind.

Though, all aspects of the problem of the employed woman are worth an analysis, it is not possible, single-handedly, to study all of them and bring forth their ramifications scientifically. So the problems arising in her familial, occupational and rural conditions are selected here for investigation and analysis.

The problems in the family are selected here for the study,

in such a way as to see how far the working woman has been relieved of her burden in the family so as to strike a balance between her two roles, home and work. "Working women face problems in their work life. These problems, it is assumed, arise out of a conflict in their dual roles. As a result, the job, the home of the woman herself suffers."[8]

The genesis of her problems lies in the maladjustment of her roles. If a working woman is too much beset with her familial obligations, she is not able to do justice to her work-role outside. If changes, in the family conducive to her role as an employee outside occur then there is every likelihood that she would be able to reconcile her two roles.

In western countries, social change has emerged in such a way as to give fillip to the western woman to work out-door. The following observation of Jephcott *et al* (1962) points out the nature of social change in the western society which helped the married woman to reconcile her both the roles. They comment, "Married Women's employment can be seen as one of the social changes resulting from smaller families, better health, improved services and lighter domestic chores."[9] The Bermondsey Study (1962)[10] which is one of the pioneering studies of its kind, of women workers with home responsibilities has put forward the facts about the women employees who have successfully evolved the technique of coping with the dual jobs. The study points out that the lighter domestic chores, husband's cooperation in the household duties, woman seeking employment after the children have reached the school age, help from relatives, use of modern labour saving gadgets etc. combined with other factors, have lessened the burden of household duties of the employed woman, and have enabled her to reconcile her two roles.

Have Indian conditions changed as to allow the Indian working woman to carry on her double roles effectively like that in the Western Society ? How far such changes have taken place in Indian family of the working woman is worth an analysis. In the present work, an attempt has been made to study such changes in the family of the employed women in villages. In the absence of such a change alluded above, the working woman will be required to carry out the entire domestic work load along with the work outside.

Such a situation may give rise to the theoretical possibility contemplated by Parsons (1952) in his analysis of the exposure of the actor to contradictory sets of role expectations. He expounds, "The exposure of the actor to conflicting sets of legitimized role expectations such that the complete fulfilment of both is realistically impossible. It is necessary to compromise, that is, to sacrifice some at least of both sets of expectations, or to choose one alternative and sacrifice the other. In any case the actor is exposed to negative sanctions."[11] In the case of employed woman there is every possibility that both of her roles and herself would suffer if she is equally exposed to both the role expectations, the complete fulfilment of which is impossible.

Employment of woman in itself is a modern phenomenon in Indian Society. Especially, in rural areas it constitutes a part of modernization, introduced deliberately. Successful performance of her occupational role, depends together with other factors, upon modernization of her family role too. If the traditional set up of the family remains the same, 'lag' is bound to occur in her two roles, which in turn would create problems of adjustment for her, as all the aspects of social system are interconnected with one another. One of the purposes of the present study is to see how far changes conducive to the work-role outside have occurred in the family of the working woman. As Karve (1966) observes about the two roles of women, "In the ultimate analysis everywhere women have to move towards establishing harmony in the domestic as well as out-door role as in the interest of the family, nation and society."[12]

Another field explored in the present work is the occupational one. Efforts are made, here to locate and analyse the employment problems of the women. The problems of employed woman arising out of her occupational sphere are studied here. The nature of relationship between the woman worker and her employing agency too, commands the attention of a researcher.

The impersonal bureaucratic structure itself creates certain problems for her as the Indian Woman is accustomed or rather socialised from her very childhood to the small primary group environment of family only. A study of her traditional roles, as a daughter, as a wife, and as a mother, clearly shows that these roles are confined to the four walls of the family group only. Hindu woman forms an integral part of her family. Her whole training and preparation for life is for this group only. Cormack' (1953) observes, "We have seen in the above material and indeed in the entire study that the whole purpose of the training and education of Hindu girls is preparation for marriage. But marriage is not the end in itself, but the means and the only means by which the family is perpetuated. It is the family that is important, that must be protected, that must be kept alive. "She exists because of the family and for the family. Therefore it is not surprising that the Hindu woman feels a strong identification of self with the family."[13]

Taking into consideration the above observations, it becomes clear that the role of employee is new one to Indian woman as her whole life is supposed to exhaust in the personal familial milieu. She is accustomed to warm, inclusive, non-utilitarian relationships of primary group only. Now, due to employment she is suddenly thrown into the matter-of-fact, exclusive, rational, impersonal, formal and utilitarian world of employment without sufficient formal or informal orientation to her new role. In such a situation, conflict is bound to ensue between primary group values and secondary group values.

In the terms of Parsons' 'Pattern variables', we can say that the occupational structure rests on universalism, performance, affective-neutrality and specificity. But here the Hindu woman more or less, throughout her life is confined to the small family environment which embodies the values of particularism, diffuseness, affectivity and quality. These two types of group values stand in contradistinction to each other. The bureaucratic structure is bound to create stresses and strains for the employed woman.

Another thing to note in this connection is that the occupational role enlarges the role set of woman. At the same time it is a new role. In such a situation, as there exists no set patterns of behaviour to adhere to in her new role set, the interaction pattern between the actor and the alter would become blurred. Such a situation is likely to be favourable for the one who is already enjoying superior status and sometimes would lead to the exploitation of the one who is in a vis-a-vis inferior position in the existing social structure.

For generations, Indian women have been relegated to inferior positions. Their entry into the 'occupational world of man' is very recent. They are not yet accepted as equals in this sphere of activity. Stereotyped notions about the sexes are still prevailent. Even today the inherent capacity of woman in handling the occupational role is always challenged. In such circumstances, the new occupational role might be weighing heavily on her. The study seeks to find out her problems in this context.

Thirdly, her problems arising out of rural conditions are studied in the present work. These employed women have to live and work in rural environment. Some of their problems owe their origin to this particular type of setting in which they have to work. The present study seeks to find out and analyse the nature of these problems.

As seen earlier, her role is mainly of an innovator. She has to work as a carrier of new ideas and values to the rural people. As a community development worker, she has to assist the women folk to accept modern ways of life, scientific outlook, new techniques, new ideas etc. She is expected to create in them urges and needs for modern ways of life and thus help them to set aside the out-moded traditional patterns of life to which they are accustomed for years together.

The employment of woman and her role are novelties to the villagers. Naturally well-defined norms and sanctions governing the interactions between the employed woman and the rural people have not yet emerged. How such situation which leads to conflict can be seen in the following observation of Crow and Crow. "In the absence of well defined social values, likelihood of conflct becomes greater.........in the period of transition one is not very certain of what is socially right and wrong and conflict cannot be avoided."[14]

All these developmental programmes are institutionalized changes. The employed woman is supposed to act as the agent of this change. Talcott Parsons' analysis of the institutionalization of Science and its application can be profitably applied in this regard too. He says, "Obviously one fundamental feature of the institutionalization of Science and its application is the introduction of a continual stream of factors of change into the social system."[15] He further says, "It is by no means to be taken for granted that because in terms of our dominant value system, scientific advance is a good thing, either the processes by which this is accomplished or the application of the results will be easily and automatically accepted. On the contrary there are many strains and resistances. Some of these are associated with the communication gap between the specialist and the 'laity', some with the special 'privileges' required by the investigator or the applied scientist, some with his interference with established ways of doing things or thinking, and some with the fact that he introduces changes which if adopted require the abandonment of established ways in which there is a vested interest."[16]

In the present context, the developmental schemes are institutionalized changes introduced in the rural community for its modernization. There is every possibility that such changes would produce continual stream of factors of change in the social system which will require readjustment of stabilized patterns of interaction. But as people develop vested interests in the existing social system, they will try to resist the deliberately introduced change.

As the agent of change the employed woman is liable to suffer from the resistance of the villagers, as the change may interfere with their established ways of doing or thinking or sometimes it may require their abandonment of established ways in which they have vested interest. So attempt is made here to find out the structural constraints present in the rural community which create difficulties for employed women and in turn blocks the process of externally stimulated and guided change. Dube's observation about the acceptance of agents of change by the community is worth mentioning here. He observes, "The acceptance of the agents of change as well as the effectiveness of the media through which they endeavour to communicate their innovations are largely governed by the cultural pre-dispositions, attitudes and social organization of the community in which they operate."[17] So the problems of the employed woman in rural areas are also studied in the context of rural community.

Theoretically, the entire phenomenon of the problems of employed women in rural community can be viewed as an illustration of the repercussions of modernization on the traditional social structure. It seems to be an aspcct of the conflict between traditional social system trying at its best not to lose the ground held for many generations and the pressure of modernization.

The present study was undertaken, though it makes no pretence to completeness to locate and analyse the problems of employed women working in rural areas. The problems emerging from familial, occupational and rural conditions are studied here. I hope the facts based on scientific inquiry would be of some value to our social policy makers and for further research.

Some Basic Queries

After Independence, the development activities for the rural areas started working speedily. So as a part of the development programme, the cadre of women workers was created for bettering the conditions of rural women-folk. Many women were recruited as employees to work in the villages.

In this context some important questions arise. Has the working woman been able to make the necessary reconciliations and accommodations to the village conditions ? Has she been prepared adequately to meet the challenge which her new position and conditions have imposed upon her ? Has the employing agency anticipated her problems while employing her ? Has the Government given any considerations to the adverse effects of her problems on the achievement of the ultimate aims of these development activities ?

If the woman is beset with insurmountable difficulties of her own, she is not able to do justice to her new role. Naturally, the very purpose for which she is sent to the village is likely to be defeated. The present study seeks to find out answers to above mentioned queries.

The objectives of the Present Industry

The problems of employed women in the urban area could catch the attention of quite a few sociologists in modern times. But the employed women in the rural areas were still neglected. So it was thought essential to study her problems and hence this study.

A number of cases of harassment of women-employees in rural areas, were reported in the newspapers and the same were discussed on the floor of Maharashtra Legislature. In the context of the various incidences of harassment of these women, the author felt that it was worthwhile to analyse their problems from a sociological perspective.

Another consideration, which induced the present researchers to undertake this study was, she felt the problems of employed woman would adversely affect the development programmes meant for the millions of people suffering from poverty, illiteracy, mal-nutrition and poor standard of public health and whose development is vitally linked with India's progress as a nation.

The objectives of the research in hand is to investigate into the problems of employed women in rural areas, analyse the factors responsible for her problems and to show how her problems affect her occupational role.

REFERENCES

1. Ministry of Community Development and Co-operation, Government of India : "Gram Sevika" (July 1960) p. 1.
2. Cormack Margaret, "The Hindu Woman" (Bureau of publticaions, Teachers College Columbia University, New York, 1953) p. viii.
3. *Ibid.* p. 185.
4. *Ibid.* p. 187.
5. Prabhu Pandharinath H., "Hindu Social Organization.", (Popular Prakashan, Bombay, 1963) p. 279.
6. Kapadia K.M., "Marriage and Family in India." (Oxford University Press, Bombay, 1966) p. 272.
7. Gadgil D.R., "Women in Working force in India." (Asia Publishing House, Bombay, 1965 (Pamphlet), p. 7.

8. Ranade S.N. and Ramachandran P., "Women and Employment." (Tata Institute of Social Sciences, Bombay, 1970.) p. 23.
9. Jephcott Pearl, "Married Women Working." (George Allen and Unwin Ltd., London, 1962) p. 135.
10. Ref. Jephcott Pearl "Married Women Working."
11. Parsons Talcott, "The Social System" (Tavistock Publications Ltd., London, 1952) p. 280.
12. Dr. Karve Iravati, "The Indian Women in 1975", (Indian Institute of Public Administration, New Delhi. 1966), p. 27.
13. Cormack Margaret, "The Hindu Woman," (Bureau of Publications, Teachers College, Columbia University, New York, 1953) p. 189.
14. A Quotation of Crow and Crow, as quoted by Dr. Promilla Kapoor in "Marriage and the Working Woman in India." (Vikas Publications New Delhi, Year, 1971) p. 11.
15. Parsons Talcott "The Social System" (Tavistock Publications Ltd., London, 1952) p. 505.
16. *Ibid.* p. 505.
17. Dube S.C. "India's Changing Villages." (Routledge and Kegan Paul Ltd., London, 1960) p. 132.

CHAPTER TWO

RESEARCH DESIGN

THIS chapter is mainly devoted to the description of the research procedure adopted for collecting data in the present study. These following points are discussed in this chapter :

1. The considerations involved in selecting the universe and the sample.
2. The technique used for data collection and the procedure followed for carrying out the actual field work.
3. Limitations of the present study.

Universe and Sampling

The study proposes to investigate and analyse the problems of employed women in rural areas. So the selection of the locale of research and of the sample was guided by the above delimitation of the problem of research.

Rural areas of Parbhani district were chosen as the locale for the present study. Parbhani district is a part of the Maharashtra State in India. "The district with an east-west extension of 128.72 kms. (80 miles) and a north-south one of 104.58 kms. (65 miles) lies between 18° 58′ and 20° 2′ N. latitude and between 76° 4′ and 77° 42′ E. longitude, with an area of 12,552.9 kms. (4,846.7 sq. miles) and a population of 12.06 lakhs. It ranks 8th in the Maharashtra State with regard to area and 17th in respect of population.

The population of the district is predominantly agricultural, industry, ccmmerce and transport claiming only a small share of it."[1] Parbhani and Hingoli are the only large towns in the district.

These following points were taken into consideration while selecting this particular locale for the present study ;

1. The district is much less urbanized than Maharashtra as a whole.[2] So it is predominantly rural in nature.
2. 86.16 percent of the total population of the district is in rural areas.[3]
3. As this part of Maharashtra is not much developed in respect of industry, commerce, transport, education etc., the process of modernization has not yet started functioning effectively. This part has still, more or less retained its traditional rural structure.

DEFINITIONS

Rural Area

A rural area has been defined in the present work as an area having no municipality or having a population below 5,000. This definition is in line with the definition of an urban area given in the Census Hand Book of Parbhani (1961). Urban area is defined there as a place which either has a municipality or is a cantonment or has been treated as a town as it has a population of over 5,000 and 75 percent or more of male workers engaged in non-agricultural occupations.[4] Naturally, places having population less than 5,000 and having no municipalities are categorized as rural here.

Employed Woman

An employed woman is defined here as one who has been gainfully employed by Government or semi-Government agencies like Zilla Parishad, Panchayat Samiti etc. Women working on daily wages or women employed by private agencies are not included here for the study.

Sampling

The selection of the sample was restricted to gainfully employed women, working in villages.

Big cities provide various types of employment opportunities to many people. But rural areas have limited employment potentials. Employed women are not found in each and every village. Considering this factor it was thought to be fruitless to adhere to any strict sampling technique. Any particular sampling technique was not contemplated due to the following reasons also :

1. The employed women in rural areas were spread over the whole district and they were transferred very often from place to place. Also it was learnt that on many occasions, the posts, specially in the remote villages, created for women employees remained vacant as women employees were found reluctant to join on duty in these villages for several reasons.
2. Certain questions in the schedule were related to the behaviour patterns of officers and villagers. So, it was presumed that some women employees might refuse to furnish the information because of the fear of possible misuse of the same inspite of assurance of secrecy was given to them.

Any strict sampling technique was not followed due to the above-mentioned reasons. However, every attempt was made to secure as large and as representative a sample as the circumstances permitted.

The entire rural population of the district comes under the jurisdiction of Zilla Parishad. So, several attempts were made by the author to secure a list of employed women in rural areas from Parbhani Zilla Parishad authorities. The author personally approached the officers of different departments of the said body to get the consolidated list of employed women. Despite several efforts in this direction, the author could not get the accurate and consolidated list of the women employees in rural areas. Then the author on her own tapped various sources and compiled a list of employed women in rural areas. The number of gainfully employed women in rural areas was roughly estimated to be 300 to 350. Out of these employed women, 163 respondents were actually secured for the interview.

A scrutiny, of the occupational categories of working women in rural areas reveals that there exist three major categories of them :

(i) Teachers

(ii) Nurses

(iii) Gram-sevikas

The present sample includes these major categories of women workers.

Here, the term teacher includes :

1. Primary school teacher
2. Secondary school teacher

The term Nurse encompasses :

1. Nurse mid-wife
2. Auxiliary Nurse-midwife
3. Family planning worker
4. Health visitor

The term Gramsevika includes :

1. Gramsevika of family and child welfare scheme for villages
2. Gramsevika employed by Panchayat Samiti.
3. Gramsevika belonging to Nutrition Scheme for villages.

The table given on p.17 shows the category-wise strength of the respondents secured as sample.

The number of women employed by private agencies was quite negligible in these villages. So, the scope of the sample was limited to the Government or semi-Government women employees. (Zilla Parishad, Panchayat Samiti etc).

TABLE 1
Category-wise Strength of Women Employees in the Sample

Categories	Strength
Nurses	57
Gramsevikas	44
Teachers	62
Total	163

Procedure followed in securing the data

Every subject thus selected as a sample unit was personally and individually interviewed on the basis of well-prepared, structured interview schedule. The subjects were requested to be candid and honest in answering the questions and their anonymity was assured. They were given an assurance that the information given by them would be treated as strictly confidential and would be used for no other purpose than that of research.

Before it was finalised, the interview schedule was pre-tested. A small number of women (Approx. 16) employed in family and child welfare department of Parbhani Panchayat, Samiti, was selected for testing it. The questions were re-framed both in the structure and in the content, whenever necessary, in the light of the above pre-testing.

The attention was paid to the following points in the preparation of the schedule.

1. The questions were framed in a simple language, so that the respondents could easily understand their meaning.
2. The questions were framed in Marathi Language which was the mother-tongue of most of the respondents.
3. Brevity of the questions was maintained to avoid confusion on the part of the respondents and to elicit exact and precise information.

4. The questions were arranged in a logical sequence so that response should slid down automatically from one question to the other.

5. A full assurance of confidence in the use of information was given to the respondents.

6. The schedule was prepared in such a way that not more than an hour would be required to finish it up and the respondents would not feel bored. Normally the interview lasted for an hour.

The order of the presentation of the questions in the schedule is as follows :

1. The first part of the schedule is devoted to the bio-data of the respondents. Questions on age, caste, education marital status etc. were included in this section. Questions regarding the general amenities in the village, are also included herein.
   These questions were included in this section with a view to examine the relationship between these variables and the problems of employed woman.

2. In the second section of the schedule, questions regarding employment problems were incorporated. Questions on motives of getting into employment, transfer, promotions, relationships with the Officers etc. were also covered in this section. These questions were set to understand the causes and the nature of her employment problems.

3. The questions regarding the familial problems of employed woman formed the third part of the schedule. Questions pertaining to the following items such as number and age of children, whether the respondent is living alone or with the family members, help from servants in household chores, co-operation from husband in domestic duties, labour-saving gadgets etc. were included in this section. These questions were set to comprehend her familial problems.

4. The fourth section of the schedule was devoted to the questions relating to the problems of employed woman which arise out of rural situation. Questions on village leader's behaviour pattern with her, her participation in village social activities, factions in the village, her knowledge of the aims of Community Development, Panchayat Raj etc., her attitude towards the job, particular difficulties encountered due to village conditions etc. formed the final part of the schedule.

Field Work

The technique, used for data collection was that of a structured interview schedule. The author personally contacted all the respondents in the sample, and carried out the interviews on the basis of completely structured schedule.

At first, how to contact the subjects in the sample was a big question before the author. However, as some of these women employees used to come to Parbhani to attend the monthly meetings held officially at the district level, the author attended these meetings. There, the author had opportunities to acquaint them with the purpose of research in hand. Later on, they were invited to the author's house so that over a cup of tea, rapport would be established between interviewer and interviewee. It was thought that such an informal contact would facilitate the process of eliciting the essential information from them.

At the beginning of the field-work very few women came on their own to furnish the necessary information. But the author repeatedly called on them at every meeting of these employees. At last they yielded to the tenacity of the research student.

Once the ice was broken, surprisingly many women came on their own, to the author's house to supply the information. Certain questions in the schedule such as 'Does your husband help you in the household chores ?' 'who controls the finances of the house etc. ?' were amusing for them and they started taking keen interest in reading the questions and answering them.

Various villages were also visited by the author to contact the employed women whom she had no opportunity to meet at the district place. Thus about 54 villages were visited. A map of Parbhani district showing the villages visited by the author is incorporated in the present work. Quite a few times the author experienced reluctance on the part of the subjects to furnish information. The author revisited these villages. No stone was left unturned to gather necessary data despite various kinds of hurdles experienced by the author. During these visits to the villages and while attending the meetings, not only the information given by the respondents was noted down but also the impressions of the villagers, officers, co-workers etc. were taken note of.

The women employees shed their former reserve about the author as a stranger, as they saw the author mixing with them freely and started confiding with her. They candidly gave answers and in turn thanked her for taking such keen interest in them and studying their problems.

For the sake of maintaining complete anonymity it was intended to mail the questionnaire. But taking into consideration the general response to this technique of social research and the educational qualifications of the respondents the author turned to the contact method, for eliciting information.

In the face to face situation, the unwilling subjects could be patiently and successfully persuaded to supply information, which they would never do otherwise. Interview enables us to know and study even those events that are not open to observation, and are known to the respondents, only. As interview provides the best method of social study the author adopted this technique of data collection.

Thus, the field work was carried out in period of two years; from October 1969 to October 1971.

Processing of data

The entire data was coded and machine processed. The use of extremely precise statistical method was never aimed at. So at first the primary tables were prepared and then the simple method of cross-tabulation was adopted.

Limitations of the study

1. The findings of this study, are based on expressed information of the respondents which may have its own limitations. The objectivity of the author is naturally circumscribed by the extent of the respondents readiness to give the real information. Possibility of hiding certain facts on the part of the respondents cannot be completely ruled out, although every possible effort had been made to elicit authentic information.
2. Some difficulties were also experienced in clarifying the purpose of the inquiry to the respondents. Many of them thought that the inquiry was directly related to some programme of solving their problems.
3. The technique for the collection of data employed by the author, was that of structured interview schedule. All the respondents were interviewed on the basis of this schedule and necessary information was collected. Therefore the generalizations and the findings of the study are limited to this technique of data-collection only.
4. The scope of this research is limited to the employed women in rural areas of Parbhani district. So, conclusions based on this study have their own limitations and can be made applicable elsewhere, with certain precautions.
5. The Primary aim of this research was to focus attention on the broader aspects of their problems, and the present study will give the base for formulating the hypothesis for further research.

REFERENCES

1. Maharashtra State, Gazetteers 'Parbhani District' (Directorate of Government Printing, Stationary and Publications, Maharashtra State, Bombay, 1967) p. 1.

2. Census of India 1961. District Census Hand Book Parbhani. (Published by the Director, Government Printing and Stationary, Maharashtra State, Bombay 4) p. 11.
3. Maharashtra State Gazetteers 'Parbhani District' (Directorate of Government Printing, Stationary and Publications, Maharashtra State, Bombay, 1967) p. 87.
4. Census of India 1961 ; 'District Census Hand Book Parbhani'. Explanatory note p. 3.

CHAPTER THREE

EMPLOYED WOMAN AND HER FAMILY

TALCOTT PARSONS observes, "There is a certain endemic potentiality of role conflict inherent in the fact that any actor has a plurality of roles, which involve differences of pattern,... These differences have to be adjusted by an ordering or allocation of the claims of the different role-expectations to which the actor is subject. This ordering occurs by priority scales, by occasion, e.g., time and place, and by distribution among alters...This allocative ordering of any given actor's role-system is often delicately balanced. Any serious alteration in one part of it may encroach on others and thus necessitate a whole series of adjustments."[1] This analysis as propounded by Parsons can very well be applied in the case of employed woman in rural areas.

In the case of employed woman, a new additional role is added over to her existing roles as housewife and mother. Thus she is subjected to plurality of role expectations which are mutually incompatible. Consequently, the delicate balance of her former familial role system is disturbed. She is exposed to plurality of roles of different nature. This may lead to role conflict, until an equilibrium is restored between different role expectations to which she is subjected. Employment of woman is in a way a recent phenomenon, especially in rural India and so proper adjustment between the new occupational role and the traditional role seems yet to be evolved. In the transitional stage, the employed woman is exposed to the conflicting sets of role expectations.

"The married working women are required to play dual roles, one as wives, mothers and housewives and the other as employees. Being subjected to dual demands of home and work, they are liable to face a crisis of adjustments.[2] "This observation of Kapoor (1971) pin points the crux of the real problems of employed woman ; especially of those who are married. (In the present survey, only sixteen women employees were unmarried and the rest were married). The crisis of adjustment of the two roles can be resolved or minimised if necessary changes take place in both the fields. The following empirical observations by Jephcott and others (1962) show that the two roles can be compatible with each other, if certain necessary changes occur in different fields ; "The Peak Freams study had demonstrated beyond question the significance of a planned time-table and a co-operative family in making it possible for the wife to undertake a dual role."[3] "Demographic and social changes have dramatically altered the daily life of the Bermondsey housewife. The marked fall in family size and in the age at which the woman has her last child, better health, improved housing and labour saving devices have all made her physical load lighter than that of any previous generation."[4] But if the family demands on the working woman would be the same as before she is bound to face a crisis of adjustment in both of her roles. This would lead to role-conflict with its attandent strains and frustrations.

The aim in this chapter is to see whether the employed woman in rural areas, has evolved an adjustment patterns in her family, so as to strike a balance between her two roles. If not, what are her problems of adjustment in the family that arise due to the addition of her work role outside ? So, the discussion in the present chapter centres around the problems of adjustment in the family of the employed woman.

Domestic Servants

According to the prevailing family role norms in India, household duties are regarded as the sole responsibility of the housewife. She is expected to be competent in cooking, in keeping the house clean, in looking after children and entertaining visitors and guests. Indian method of cooking is time-consuming and laborious. Even preliminary preparations of cooking such as cleaning the grains and vegetables, grinding, mixing etc. take a lot of time and energy of the house wife. Looking after children is her major responsibility. She has to bathe them, keep them clean, feed them and carry the small ones everywhere with her. The child is always at the apron-string of the mother. Entertaining guest is always a big job in India. A good housewife has also to be a good host. She has to show a good sense of hospitality both to maintain the dignity of the guest and the prestige of the family. Showing negligence and disrespect to the guest is regarded as Adharma. The Hindus have a tradition to equate the guest with God. At the cost of personal inconvenience, time and energy, one has to be courteous to the guest. To make the matter worse, the guests usually do not observe general etiquettes of giving pre-intimation while visiting the houses of other people. Dropping in at odd hours and without prior intimation is more a rule than an exception. To frown upon guest is regarded as a violation of the duty of housewife. In addition to these duties, the housewife has to clean the house and manage the other household work. All these responsibilities in the house constitute a heavy work-load for the housewife. The household duties are also to be carried out in an unfavourable conditions. Sengupta (1960) aptly describes the situation when she says, "Domestic chores are performed in miserable conditions making women's work arduous and long."[5]

Employed woman is required to fulfil these role expectations more or less and along with it carry out the duties as an employee outside. In such a situation the employed housewife requires some help in household chores to lighten her burden in this respect, because her work role inevitably encroaches on her time and energy appropriately allocated to the housewife's role. One of the ways of lessening her burden in the house is to employ servants. It is a common observation that in cities, employed women quite often resort to this way to lessen the burden of their work in the house. So the inquiry was carried out to examine the situation in the case of employed woman in rural areas in this respect.

Table 2 shows that most of the respondents in the

study do not have servants to help them in their household chore. Out of 163 respondents 114 (70.1 percent) have not employed any domestic servant at all. 26 (15.95 percent) respondents have employed servants only for cleaning utensils and washing clothes. 10 (6.13 percent) women employees have servants for cleaning utensils only. From the table it appears clear, that very few women employees have employed servants for looking after children, for cooking purpose and for similar other purposes.

TABLE 2

Women Employees Hiring Domestic Servants

Items for which servants are employed.	No. of respondents.	%
1. No servant	114	70.1
2. Cleaning utensils and washing clothes	26	15 95
3. Cleaning utensils	10	6.13
4. Cleaning utensils and looking after children	5	3.06
5. Cleaning utensils, washing clothes and cooking	3	1.84
6. Washing clothes	2	1.22
7. Looking after children	2	1.22
8. Cooking	1	0.61
Total	163	

The above table clearly reveals that a considerably large number of women employees have to carry out household duties without any assistance from servants. This fact needs a detailed analysis for its proper understanding. It seems to have different social connotations.

Firstly, the problem of servants for domestic purposes seems to have its association with the ideas of occupational hierarchy in Indian villages. Domestic servants have very low social prestige. An individual working as a household servant loses his social esteem in the eyes of his fellowmen. So the villager thinks it below dignity to work as a domestic servant. Many respondents in the present inquiry complained that it becomes difficult to get servants for domestic purposes. Many respondents said that people, even from very poor section show their reluctance to work as domestic servants. One respondent said, "In villages we find dire poverty. For many people, it becomes difficult to keep the wolf from the door. Still they don't like to work as servants in other's houses. They prefer to work as farm labourers or to do some odd jobs. Dignity is more important to them."

Second the caste element seems to have some bearing on this problem. Even though in the wake of industrialization caste restrictions have been softened in the cities resulting into much more free social intercourse among the people of different castes and creeds, yet the village India presents a different picture. In rural India, there is still a strong-hold of caste institution. The feeling of superiority still persists in the minds of the people of so-called higher castes. The notions of purity and pollution still have significance for the caste Hindus. So the higher caste Hindu would never accept to work as domestic servants for the people of lower castes. So naturally the employed woman would never get any body from the caste higher than that of her own caste to work as a servant.

In this situation she is left with two alternatives to employ the servant either from her caste or from any lower caste. The people belonging to the same caste or sub-caste, living in a linguistic area are mostly each other's near or distant relatives. So they regard each other as socially equal. Master-servant relationship implies status inequality. So, persons of the same caste or sub-caste think it derogatory to work in each others houses as servants. They feel it damaging to their social prestige. So the employed woman is unable to find servants of her caste or of castes of equal ranks with her caste.

The other alternative for the employed woman is to hire servants of lower castes. Sometimes people belonging to the traditionally lower castes are sometimes willing to work as servants in the houses of higher castes. But the caste rules restrict one's commensuality with the people of lower castes. If one employes a servant of lower caste, one is likely to be denounced by the people of one's own caste for violating caste restrictions, because ideas of purity and polution still govern the close inter-relationships between different castes. If the employed woman hires the lower caste persons as domestic servants her caste members, especially the woman members would avoid going to her house and take tea, water etc. It is a common observation, that women in village India are more orthodox in following caste restrictions than men. If the employed woman hires a servant of a lower caste, she is likely to lose membership in the inner circles of her caste. One has to take into consideration the caste norms while employing a servant. It is common thing in Indian villages to ask about the caste of a person while hiring him as a servant.

These employed women themselves do not seem to have come up above caste considerations. Many respondents told me that they themselves do not like to have servants of lower castes as it sometime interferes with the performance of religious rituals. (The data in the inquiry indicate that most of these women employees are religious minded. Please see Table 6).

Thirdly, the causes of non-availability of servants can be traced in the occupational structure of the village and in the division of labour prevalent in the village. Most of the able bodied men are engaged in agriculture or allied occupations. So men will not be available as servants for household purposes. Household work such as cleaning the house, looking after children, cooking, cleaning the utensils etc. is regarded as the domain of the woman. So, men will not like to work as domestic servants. They think it below their dignity to work in this way. To work as a domestic servant, is always regarded as the last choice for the man to earn a living.

Women in villages not only do all the household work by themselves but help their men in agricultural work. So, little leisure is left for them to work as domestic servants.

Even young boys or girls, say, of ten or twelve years are also not available as servants. This fact was brought to light by many respondents. These youngsters either go to school or do some petty work with their parents or look after their young siblings. So, they too rarely work as servants.

Fourthly, it was revealed in the discussion with the women employees that they themselves were not psychologically motivated to employ servants for their domestic work. The traditional ideal of womanhood enforces a woman to be a good housewife first, and that can happen only when she does whole of her household work herself. A woman who neglects her household duties becomes an object of ridicule. So, every good house wife is expected to show interest in household work and even the employed woman is no exception to it. So, in order to avoid social criticism and win a word of praise, employed woman of lower middle class may be preferring to bear the whole household burden by herself. Can it be explained in terms of Grosser's 'role-self' theory ? Grosser has distinguished behaviour that contributes to role validation in two ways : as "role expressive" and "role supportive". "It assumes an actor who is trying to tell somebody something or to prove something. More fitting than the language of ends and means is the language of message and the symbols that convey it, or of claims and evidence...the art of seduction may be cultivated not because it is an alternative means to the goal of sexual satisfaction, but because the successful practice of the art validates a claim to being a certain sort of person."[6] Grosser's 'role-self' theory suggests one way of looking at deviance. But here, we can apply it in respect of conformity to norms also. Why is employed woman not psychologically motivated to employ domestic servants ? Is the woman employee trying to prove that she is still a housewife inspite of her employment ? Is she making an effort to proclaim herself a certain kind of self which is socially acclaimed ? Is she trying to validate her claims to the status of housewife ?

Fifthly, cultural norms in villages about certain household duties may be one of the intervening factors in respect of servants. In villages, norms about child care are such that it is the mother who has to look after the children ; she should carry them wherever she moves. It is a common sight in villages, that mothers working in fields carry their children there. A woman leaving her young child to the care of a servant and going out for work is regarded as selfish and one going after money. The data on servants too, throw light on this. Only 7 women have employed servants for minding the children (Table 2). During her visits to these villages, the author too, observed that these women employees used to carry their children to their work-places, such as schools, offices etc. It seemed that they did not mind the disturbance caused by these children at the work place. This explains why the servants are not employed to look after the children.

Sixthly, the employment of woman in rural areas is a recent phenomenon. The demand for domestic servants in the employed woman's house is of recent origin. Formerly, there would not have been such demand for servants. It would be difficult to get skilled servants immediately when the demand for them arises.

These are the different social connotations of the servants problem. Any how, the net result is that the employed woman has to pull on without the help of servants. In this way there is no significant change in her traditional role as a housewife.

Modern Labour Saving Devices

Modern labour saving devices have revolutionised the kitchen in western countries and have proved a real boon to the working wives. In the present inquiry, the data were gathered about labour saving and time saving gadgets used by the employed woman. The purpose was to see, how far the working woman is saving her time and energy in home-making for the sake of her dual roles. But to the author's surprise, the sample revealed that not a single woman was using all or some or any one of the modern labour and energy saving tools of home making such as gas ovens, pressure cooker, electric mixer-grinder, washing mechine, vacuum cleaner, refrigerator etc.

The traditional time consuming, monotonous, tiresome patterns of household chores were followed by all except none e.g. cooking was mainly done on mud 'chulhas' wherein wood was used as fuel. Washing clothes mixing the cooking ingradients, cleaning the house, washing utensils etc. were done in the same old traditional fashion. There was no modernization as such of kitchen chores. This clearly reveals that there is no lessening of the burden of the work of the housewife who is employed outside. She is still burdened with the work in the house as her mother or grandmother who was not employed. The traditional pattern of Indian housekeeping is such that home making and management take much of her time. The preparation of food, cleaning the kitchen, cleaning grains etc. are time consuming and the housewife has little time left for her own purposes. As the labour saving modern gadgets have not found their way into her kitchen. Her household work has remained significantly unchanged. She seems to be struggling hard under the same old environment.

Firstly, these women who are mostly from lower middle classes, are not yet enough motivated to leave off the traditionalism in kitchen and to adopt modern attitudes and approach towards these gadgets. Truly in cities, these gadgets have entered into the kitchens of well-to-do housewives and highly educated, salaried women employees. But the employed women in rural areas are not still convinced of the utility of these gadgets. Quite a few of these respondents had expressed their genuine doubts about the working of these devices. Many of them, opined that the old ways of home-making are better than modern ways. Many a respondent told that they did not like food cooked in cooker, or cooked on kerosene stoves. They preferred food prepared on chulhas. Most of the respondents were unanimous in their opinion that food cooked in cooker or on stove or gas oven is tasteless. Many added that even their family members also did not relish food cooked in modern ways. Thus in this respect too, stereotyped notions still prevail.

Secondly, some respondents said that as they were not used to these gadgets, it would be difficult for them to handle them. As these devices were new, some respondents thought that they require delicate, careful handling and at times the use of modern gadgets would be dangerous. So, they preferred old ways of house-keeping.

Thirdly, discussion with these women about the gadgets revealed, that these women are not accustomed to use of such gadgets. The use of them may require change in their old habits of home making. Generally, people are reluctant to change their old patterns of doing, in exchange of something of which they are not sure. This might be one of the causes for the absence of modern domestic gadgets in the house of these employed women.

Fourthly, an economic factor also needs to be taken into consideration in this context. Labour saving domestic appliances such as pressure cooker, electric mixer, electric washing machine, and the like are regarded as luxury articles by the Government and so they are heavily taxed. Consequently, prices of these articles are beyond the means of middle class people. So, it might have been difficult for these women to buy these gadgets.

Fifthly, facilities for repairing these are not available in villages. Indian villages are still technologically backward. In cities, employed women are assured of the availability of spare parts and repairing facilities for these gadgets and so they can make use of some of these labour saving devices. But in this respect employed women in rural areas are put in an unfavourable situation.

It can be included from above discussion that no major change has taken place in the kitchen of these women. They have to do the same household duties like any other Indian Woman. In such a situation, there is every likelihood that she would face the problem of articulating her different roles in a balanced way. This would create strain for her. Unless an equilibrium is restored between different role expectations, either or both of her role performances are likely to be affected adversely.

Help from Relatives

The foregoing discussion on servants and modern gadgets has clearly revealed that the employed woman in rural areas is not fortunate enough in getting sufficient assistance from servants or labour saving devices in running the home. So, the inquiry was carried out to see whether she gets help from her relatives.

Table 3, indicates that 107 out of 163 *i.e.* 65.6 percent of women employees, pull on their household work without the help from relatives. Only 56 (34.64 percent) respondents have their relatives, staying with them and helping them.

TABLE 3

Relatives in the Family at the Place of Job

Whether living with relatives	Number of women employees	
		%
Living with relatives	56	34.35
No relatives at the place of job	107	65.64
Total	163	

When certain questions were asked about relatives, the respondents expressed the problem in the following manner. One respondent said, "Relatives have their own familial obligations. They have to look after their school going children or younger ones, and to attend to the needs of their husbands. So, they find it difficult to come over here to a far-off place leaving their families. Even our younger brothers or sisters don't like to come to the villages as they have their schools or colleges to attend. Another respondent said, "Grown up younger sisters are usually of much help in the household chores and in looking after children. But parents don't like to send unmarried daughters to the villages because they have heard so much about molestation of women employees in villages." Another one responded, "If we would have stayed in the same place or in the same town or village where our relatives stay or near our native place, we would have received the help of relatives. But who is going to come to such distant places ?" Another said, "village life is drab and dreary. There is no excitement, no entertainment as in cities. That is the reason why our relatives don't like to come to the village. One more respondent said, "we ourselves are fed up with the humdrum life in the village. But any way we have to stay on here. Then why we should trouble our relatives by bringing them here ?" Many respondents said that they are often transferred from place to place anywhere in Maharashtra. So, their relatives find it difficult to move with them wherever they go and to adjust themselves there.

In olden days, when the family was a joint unit, relatives used to help each other. But the date in the present inquiry shows that 65.6 percent of these women live without relatives in the house. Most of these women have come from cities or towns. So, does the absence of relatives reflect the thinning of kinship bond in modern times, which used to be very strong in the traditional Indian Society ? Or, is there any situational factor to account for this phenomenon ?

The Bermondsey[7] case study of the employed woman has illustrated that, if the help from relatives is available, the employed woman is in a better position to reconcile her two roles. This study has shown that the employed woman in Bermondsey Community, safely entrusts the minding of the children to her mother or married daughter who stays nearby. Thus she can take the help of relatives whenever she requires because they all stay nearby each other. But it is revealed in our study, that here the employed woman in rural areas is usually transferred from place to place, and finds it difficult to get the help from her relatives.

In India, close relatives form a strong primary group. They help each other in adversities and on many social and religious occasions, they form a strong informal social group. But this is so, only if they live in neighbourhood. But, if the relatives stay far apart from each other, it becomes difficult for them to help each other. Staying, amidst relatives gives a sense of security to the person. Many respondents said that they feel insecure as they have to live in a strange place far away from their near relatives. This feeling of insecurity may be causing more strain to the employed woman. And it is likely to result in deviation from some of the expectations of one or both of the roles on the part of the woman employee.

TABLE 4
Husband's Co-operation in Household Work

Items in which Husband's co-operation was available	Number of women getting co-operation	%
Domestic chores (Such as cooking cleaning the house etc.)	NIL	
Looking after children	16	9.81
Guidance in occupation	43	26.38
Looking after children and Guidance in occupation	12	7.36
Co-operation in domestic chores, looking after children and guidanee in occupation	17	10.42
No co-operation in any of these items	18	11.04
Not applicable	57	34.96
Total	163	

Husband's Co-operation

One can discern from the earlier discussion that the employed woman is not able to get the help from servants, labour saving devices and also from relatives. Then naturally the question is as to how she manages the dual roles. Does she get help from her husband in home-making ? The data were collected about husband's help. A scrutiny of the above table reveals that the husband's share in the domestic work as such is almost nill. But they would guide their working wives in their official work. Some of the respondents said that their husbands co-operate in looking after the children. Questions were put in the inquiry to the employed woman to delineate in detail her husband's co-operation in looking after children. But it could be ascertained from their replies that for them, looking after children meant only taking the children out or playing with them occasionally or general supervision. Looking after children did not mean complete care of children such as bathing them, cleaning them or feeding them etc. These duties about children are regarded as the sole responsibilities of the mother only.

It is possible for her to combine both the roles if her husband shares household chore with her. This has been amply proved in the Bermondsey study, "The husband on the other hand assisted on the grand scale. He not only undertook the traditional man's job of house decorating and repairs but gave a very considerable hand in the daily round of washing up and cleaning grates. In addition, he frequently made himself responsible for such regular tasks as window cleaning, floor polishing, ironing and turning out a room. His domestic help was not only extensive, even more important from the wife's point of view, it was dependable."[8] "The Peak Freams study showed that when the wife worked on the evening shift, it was the husband who regularly undertook the care of the children."[9]

But our data here revealed that the Indian condition seems to be different in this respect. The fact may be explained by analysing husband-wife relationship as existing in India. Dube says, "According to the traditional norms of society, a husband is expected to be authoritarian figure, whose will should always dominate the domestic scene.... The husband is superior ; the wife is his subordinate."[10] "She has to spend the whole day in considering matters entirely related to the house and was particularly to be attentive to the needs and desires of her lord, always subordinating her own comforts and convenience to his."[11] "On the whole, however, the traditional outlook on husband-wife relationship is still so strong in India that it may be long before the more equalitarian ideal becomes a part of the natural expectations of marriage. In the recent study, Desai found that although some Hindu women objected strongly to the complete obedience expected of them by their husbands, the large majority accepted the older concept of their subordinate position."[12]

Thus husband enjoys superior status in the family. It is but natural that he would be reluctant to do household work which carries low prestige as well as which is considered as a woman's job. As Ross puts it, "Women's task in all societies have less prestige than those of men, women taking over male business or professional roles are moving to a higher level of job prestige, whereas men are moving to a lower level of work."[13]

As the husband enjoys superior position, he may think working in the house as not befitting his stature.

In India, by tradition wife is supposed to be dependant on her husband in all respects. So, certain prejudices emerge about the working woman and her family. If a woman works outside, it is regarded that her husband is not capable of affording her and the family. So, he is held in low esteem by the people. The husband is conscious of this as he is socialised in the same society and must have internalised the same norms and values. Wife working outside may be hurting his ego. Does non-co-operation by husband in home making, reflects his psychological reaction of over asserting his superiority which is supposed to be threatened due to wife's working outside ?

Even from wife's point of view husband's household work doing is not regarded a proper. The questions in the schedule regarding husband's participation in the household matters drew amusing and surprising remarks from many of the respondents. One respondent said, "We ourselves don't like even the idea of making husband work in the house and his being ridiculed as henpecked by fellowmen." Another respondent said, "A husband is always superior to his wife. We cannot entertain even the idea of a husband working in the house like a woman.' One respondent said, "How can he be able to work in the house when he is not habituated to this sort of work before, in his life ?"

A question was included in the schedule to see whether the employed women expect the husband to work in the home. Almost all married respondents said that they don't expect their husbands to work in that way. People ridicule the woman whose husband does household duties. The woman then, is regarded as not playing her role of housewife properly. The norms of the society in this respect prohibit and discourage her to take such help from him. This might be one of the reasons why women don't expect their husbands to help them in the household chores.

Even though, the status of wife is considered inferior to that of her husband, she occupies an important position in the house. She is indispensable to the family. She has functional importance for the family as she does the entire household work. Naturally she gains certain position in the family. When the employed woman says that she never expects husband's participation in household chores, does it reflect her fear that husband's participation may encroach on her long established indispensable position in the family ? Does she feel that her importance in the family will be lessened due to husband's sharing household work ?

In India, after Independence, there is no dejure discrimination between the sexes. Men and women are equal before law. But *de facto* change about the equality of women is yet to emerge. At present, especially in villages, there is no significant change in the relationship between husband and wife. Still the husband is regarded socially superior to his wife. The egalitarian values of modernization about the sexes in social matters are yet to be accepted in India. The social change is lagging far behind in this respect. Even though the woman is employed, the norms relating to the traditional division of labour still persist. Household work is not regarded as an act of partnership between husband and wife. Even to-day, children continue to be socialised mainly in a traditional way for the family roles. In such a situation, help from husband in home making is too much to expect.

Mother of Young Children

As a mother of small children, some of the employed women found the task of working outside very difficult as young children require constant attention from them. The following table reveals 83 married women have children below 6 years of age.

TABLE 5

Employed Women and Age of their Children

Age of Children	Number of employed women	%
6 and below 6 years	83	50.92
Above 6 years	42	25.96
Not applicable	38	23.31
Total	163	

The data in the above table reveals that the number of employed women having small children is considerably large. The reconciliation of the two roles become very difficult when the woman has to attend every now and then to the needs of her small children who are very small. Dr. Kapoor rightly points out this situation in the following words, "But the working wife, especially if she has children, will have to make in many instances, a little greater effort to keep things going and she needs more help than is commonly given to her."[14] The following quotation also shows how much developed countries do for the working mother anticipating their double strain, "The Soviet Union virtually expects every woman in the labour force as well as home maker, but it provides her with great amount of help in the form of nurseries for small children, and a widely extended health services for example. The Kibbuiz of Israel carried this even further by virtually taking complete care and control of the children away from the mother except for a few hours of the day."[15]

But in the present research, it was observed that the employed woman has to carry heavy work-load in house as she does not get any help from servants, from labour saving gadgets, from relatives or from husband. In addition, most of the women have to look after their small children. This causes heavy strain on the working woman.

Employment of woman is a recent phenomenon in villages.

So there are no such facilities as such for child care as are available in some of the cities. In big cities the matter is different. Large number of women employees are concentrated in cities. So, it becomes possible for them to get day nursery, baby sitting facilities and the like.

Another thing to note in this connection is that certain convictions are prevalent about child care in villages. Children are supposed to be the gifts of God. They should never be neglected. Specially the mother is held responsible for the well being of the child. The mother carries the child wherever she moves. It is a usual practice for the mother. If the woman neglects the child, she is regarded as selfish. Children are regarded as the real wealth of the family. A married woman in village is usually greeted with a question, inquiring a number of children she has. This shows the importance given to the children in villages. One saying about children is often heard from the women in the villages, "Who will ask you how rich you are but certainly there will be a question about the number of children you have. They constitute the real wealth." These norms about children might be putting a heavy strain on the working women.

Many times it was seen, while interviewing these women that even these employed women themselves were found reluctant to leave their children in the care of their servants or other persons. On the contrary, they felt a severe sense of guilt of neglecting their children due to their employment, even if occasionally, it compelled them to be away from children. The following incidents bring this point in the proper perspective. One respondent was a teacher working in a primary school. She had one year old child. In the interview when the question was asked to her "Who looks after the child when you go to school ?" She suddenly broke into tears and after some time in a challenging mood said, "The head master of my school is not allowing me to bring my child to the school. He says, it disturbs the school. Has he no children of his own ? Is he brought up without his mother looking after him ? Who will look after my child when I go to the school ?"

Another incident is of a gramsevika. Before coming to Parbhani district she was working in a village in Jalgaon district of Maharashtra. There she was staying with her husband and as that was her native district, occasionally relatives used to come to help her in needs. But one day she received the order of her transfer to a village in the Parbhani District. She was ordered to join the duty immediately at the new place. One has to walk two miles to reach this village from the nearest station. As the area was unknown to her and as the child was unwell, she had to leave the child with her husband and come to join her duty alone in the village. When the question was asked about the neglect of children, the woman was virtually in tears so much so that, for some time she was unable to utter a single word as her voice was choked with emotions. She said, "What did they get by transferring me like this ? My child is breast-fed and is unwell. My breasts are full now. It is agonising physically even. Does it mean that employed women should not have children ?"

Dr. Mrs. Iravati Karve makes two categories of women workers and hints at the difficulty which the mother of small children finds in reconciling her both the roles, (a) "Single woman, or married woman returning to work after their children have grown up. (b) Mother of young children who require to be looked after. In the interest of both mothers and their children the trend in developed countries is to create conditions in which women falling under category (b) are not compelled to seek employment at the cost of domestic responsibility."[16]

Mrs. C. Hate too, expresses doubts about the reconciliation of the two roles by the women when the children are small. "It becomes a great problem to arrange for the proper care of the children and at the same time to attend to the duties at the prescribed time. If children are grown up, well and good. Otherwise to entrust them to servants for a long time is not in their interest. On her return from full time job quite exhausted how far a woman will be able to pay due attention to the children is a question."[17]

In western countries, it seems, mothers with a child under five do not seek employment outside, under normal circumstances. In the study 'Married, women working', Pearl Jephoti and others point out this fact. "Since the mother with a child under five worked in exceptional circumstances only, the problem of child care was chiefly connected with the children of school age."[18]

But in the present research, many women employees were seen having children below six years of age. So it may be inferred from the above discussion that the working women in rural areas, have to carry out a heavy load of domestic reponsibilities along with her work outside.

Religious Rituals

Another problem which the Hindu married employed woman faces is that, as a married woman she has to perform various religious rituals or vratas which consume a lot of her time and energy. This too constitutes one more problem. An inquiry was conducted to see whether the employed woman has made some alterations in her religious practices to harmonise her double roles.

TABLE 6

Performance of Religious Rituals

Response	Number of Women	%
Yes	70	42.94
It is difficult, still performed due to religious pressure	77	47.23
No	16	9.81
Total	163	

The above table clearly reveals continued religious conservatism among the employed women. The Table indicates 147 out of 163 *i.e.*, 90.1 per ecnt of women employees fulfil religious obligations.

A Hindu married woman has to perform various religious rituals. The ideal of Pativrata is entrenched in many of the religious rituals, as husband is the centre of all her activities and interests in life. From her very childhood Hindu woman is socialized in this respect. So she dreads even to the idea of widowhood. Many rituals such as Vatpurnima, Makarsankranti etc. are performed for wishing a long life for husband. Some of the vratas or rituals are connected with the continuation of family traditions. They are called 'Kulavratas'. A woman is supposed to be the custodian of family traditions. This is more so in modern times as men have left many of the rituals to be performed by womem in the house. The married woman is supposed to perform these rituals. There are various festivals and ceremonies among Hindus. For every festival and ceremony there are corresponding religious rituals. The responsibility of preliminary preparations of these rituals and many times of the actual performance of these rituals fall on women.

Another thing to note in this connection is that not only worshipping the Gods is supposed to be her duty, but she has to cook special dishes which are ordained by religious scriptures. Preparation of these special dishes takes a lot of time and energy.

The ideas about these religious rituals are so deep-rooted in the minds of women that inspite of admitting that the religious rituals are burdensome, they strictly adhere to them. One respondent said, "On some of the holy days, I observe fast. On these days with hungry stomach, it becomes difficult for me to work outside, specially when on tours." Another respondent said, "By profession I am a nurse. But being a Brahmin and a married woman I have to perform several religious rituals at home. As a nurse I have to touch the bodies of persons belonging to various castes. So when I come home I take bath and then prepare the food required for the rituals and then I worship God. Whatever may be the hardships, how to forget one's own Dharma." Another respondent said, "This bread is given by God. How could I to forget Him ? Ultimately it is one's religious merit that matters." Many of the respondents were surprised even at the question on religious rituals. Performance of religious rituals by married women and old people is taken for granted in India.

Another facet of this problem is that a woman incurs censure from her caste and family members if she fails to perform religious rituals. And sometimes she may lose informally, her membership in her close caste/kinship group. It is also possible that she would get scolding from elderly members in the family if she neglects religious duties.

The traditional outlook of marriage as a sacrament is still prevalent, "Marriage was desired not so much for sex or progeny, as for obtaining a partner for the fulfilment of one's religious duties...... the basic aim of the marriage was Dharma."[19] This outlook may be a cause of why the married woman performs several religious rituals not minding the difficulties and strains involved in it.

From the data, it is clear that the employed women have to carry on the religious obligations like any other woman. This situation is bound to create role conflict in her. Her role as an employee is bound to suffer if she carries on all her former role obligations, without sufficient alterations in them.

Service hours

The analysis hitherto given, highlights the facts that the employed woman has to carry out the burden of heavy household work. There are no significant alterations as such in her former role system of housewife. So, the inquiry was conducted to see whether she has less working hours outside so that, no formidable change, in her former role system may be required. The data are as follows.

It can be inferred from the Table 7 that almost all the women employees have to work outside the house for not less than 4 hours a day. The table shows that 60 women have to work for 8 hours a day. 53 women work for 6 hours a day and 24 women work for 5 hours a day. These working hours are too heavy a burden for a woman who has to shoulder the entire responsibility of her household work.

There are well-established norms and sanctions for the role of a housewife. The primary duty of a woman is regarded as that of a housewife. But this is not the case with her occupational

TABLE 7
Service Hours Outside

Hours of Work	Number of Women employees	%
Less than 4 hours work	1	0.61
4 hours	11	6.74
5 hours	24	14.72
6 hours	53	32.51
7 hours	6	3.68
8 hours	60	36.80
9 hours	4	2.45
10 hours	—	0.00
No definite hours	4	2.45
Total	163	

role. This role is new. The clearcut norms and sanctions for her occupational role are yet to emerge. So there is every possibility that the employed woman would lean more towards her familial role, and consequently, her occupational role would suffer, or there would be a conflict between her two roles, which would result in her departure from an ideal conformity to both of her roles.

Role Conflict

As noted earlier, Parsons says, "There is a certain endemic potentiality of role conflict, inherent in the fact, that any actor has a plurality of roles which involves differences of pattern." In the employed woman's case, her two roles involve differences of patterns of behaviour. So, there is every possibility that role conflict will ensue. So the question was included in the schedule to ascertain the role conflict, if any. The question was whether she feels that the children and husband are neglected due to her job. The following are the data gathered.

TABLE 8
Feel Negligence towards Children and Husband due to Job

Response	Number of Women	%
Feel children and husband Neglected	101	61.96
Don't feel neglected	50	30.67
Not definite	12	7.36
Total	163	

To comprehend her attitude towards job and the household duties, another question was included in the schedule. This question was about her preference for job or household duties. The following are the data collected.

TABLE 9
Preference for Job or Household Duties

Response	Number of Women	%
Prefer job	98	60.12
Prefer household duties	33	20.24
Equal preference to both	27	16.56
No preference	5	3.06
Total	163	

An inspection of the above tables reveals that almost equal number of women say that they feel that the children and husband are neglected due to job and at the same time they say that they prefer job to household duties. This is clearly an indication of role conflict. The analysis of this role conflict can be presented in the following words of Dr. Kapoor, "Tension is felt mainly because she feels torn between her loyalty towards her husband and children. She wants to devote time equally seriously to both and in trying to be efficient in both these spheres finds herself torn and tired. She suffers from a guilt sense when owing to her job she neglects her child, husband or home but she equally suffers if she neglects her office work."[20] That role conflict is an obvious source of strain and frustration for an individual is pointed out by Parsons in the following words. He says, "Exposure to role conflict is an obvious source of strain and frustration in that it creates a situation incompatible with a harmonious integration of personality with the interaction system. There must be external frustrations, internal conflicts or both, in the severer cases always both. Indeed what, on the interaction level if not the fully developed social role level, is exposure to conflicting expectations of some kind may be presumed to be the generic situation underlying the development of ambivalent motivational structures with their expression in neuroses, in deviant behaviour or other-wise."[21] That the employed woman faces acute problems of adjustment in the family is clear from the data in the inquiry.

Summary

The familial problems of employed women in rural areas have been discussed at length so far. No servants to help, no modern gadgets to save labour and time, no help from relatives or husband, responsibility of young children, pressure of religious rituals and full time job outside the house are her main problems. That the woman is subjected to role conflict is clearly seen in the inquiry. Her problems in the family and the role conflict to which she is subjected to, are clear indications of strain on her.

The occupational role of woman necessitates a whole series of adjustments in her former familial role-system so as to reconcile both the role expectations. But the study has revealed that the emergence of occupational role of the woman, employed in rural areas has not been accompanied by the necessary changes in her former role system. And here lies the genesis of her problems.

REFERENCES

1. Parsons, Talcott, "The Social System" (Tavistock Publications Ltd., London, 1952) pp. 280-281.
2. Dr. Kapoor, Promilla, "Marriage And The Working Woman In India" (Vikas Pub. New Delhi, 1971) p. 12.
3. Jephcott Pearl J. and Others, "Married Women Working" (George Allen and Unwin Ltd. London, 1962) p. 92.
4. *Ibid.*, p. 166.
5. Sengupta Padmini, "Women Workers of India" (Asia Publishing House, Bombay, 1960) pp. 273-74.
6. Albert K. Cohen, "Deviance and Control" (Prentice-Hall of India Private Limited, New Delhi, 1970) p. 102.
7. Please refer, Jephcott Pearl *et. al.* "Married Women Working" (George Allen & Unwin Ltd., London, 1962).
8. *Ibid.*, p. 167.
9. *Ibid.*
10. Quotation of Dr. S. C. Dube, mentioned by Dr. Kapoor Promilla in "Marriage and the Working Woman" (Vikas Pub. New Delhi, 1971) p. 9.
11. *Ibid.* (Quotation of Indira) p. 9.
12. Ross D. Aileen, "The Hindu Family in its Urban Setting" (University of Toronto Press, Bombay 1966) p. 107.
13. *Ibid.*, p. 87.
14. Dr. Kapoor, Promilla, "Marriage and the Working Woman" (Vikas Pub. Delhi 6).
15. Quotation of Paul Popenone mentioned by Dr. Kapoor Promilla in "Marriage and the Working Woman" (Vikas Pub. New Delhi, 1971) p. viii.
16. Dr. Karve. Iravati, "The Indian Women in 1975" (The Indian Institute of Public Administration, Indraprastha Estate, New Delhi) p. 9.
17. Hate, Chandrake A., "Hindu Woman and her future" (New Book Company Limited, Bombay, 1948) p. 227.

18. Jephcott, Pearl *et, al.*, "Married Women Working" (George, Allen and Unwin Ltd,. London 1962) p. 168.

19. Kapadia, K.M. "Marriage and family in India," (Oxford University Press, Bombay. 1966) pp. 167-168.

20. Dr. Kapoor, Pramilla, "Marriage & the Working Woman in India" (Vikas Pub. New Delhi, 1971) p. 309.

21. Parsons Talcott, "The Social System" (Tavistock Publications Ltd., London, 1952) p. 282.

CHAPTER FOUR

EMPLOYED WOMAN AND WORK

THE ANALYSIS in the last Chapter has pin-pointed the familial problems of employed woman in rural areas. The aim in this chapter is to investigate and analyse her problems in the occupational field.

In India, the entry of the woman in the occupational world of man is a recent one. The employment of women particularly in rural areas is a very recent phenomenon. As this occupational role is new one, it is bound to create problems of adjustment. Uptil now, the world of the woman was circumscribed by the family group. So, she was socialised mainly for her family roles only. Now she, as well as, the society have to learn to accommodate her in her new role. Until the adjustment is evolved in her new situation, she has to face the uncertainties accompanying the new role, until some measure of adjustment is evolved in her new situation.

That the occupational role of woman creates problems of adjustment is clear from the following observation of Aileen Ross. She observes, "Each new occupational role taken over by women, creates problems of adjustment of attitude and behaviour. The opposition to the people playing new roles is caused by the uncertainty not only of the incumbent in the unfamiliar situation, but also of those who play related roles."[1] The impressions of Aileen Ross about the employed women in India, are also worth noting in this context. She says, "She may have to work outside the home to augment the family income. If so, she adds another role to her repertoire, one which at the present stage of women's position in India, is so uncharter that it entails all the uncertainties of a pioneer job."[2]

The new occupational role creates problems of adjustment for working woman. So, here an attempt is made in this chapter to delineate the occupational problems of employed woman in rural areas and analyse the factors responsible for her problems. The following discussion centres around this aim.

New Role

A scrutiny of the following data reveals that the employment of woman in rural areas is a recent phenomenon. Table 10 about age group distribution of respondent shows that 125 women out of 163 are under 35 years of age. It shows 76 percent of women employees belong to young age category (18-35 yrs). This can be corroborated with the data in Table 11 about the number of years of experience of service of these respondents. The data in this table show that 70.5 percent of women employees have less than eight years' experience in service.

TABLE 10

Age-group Distribution of the Employed Women

Age-group	Number of Women	%
18-20 yrs.	4	2.45
21-25 yrs.	53	32.51
26-30 yrs.	45	27.60
31-35 yrs.	27	16.56
36-40 yrs.	17	10.42
Above 40	17	10.42
Total	163	

TABLE 11
Experience of Service

Years	Number of respondents	%
Less than one year's service	5	3.06
1 to 2 years' service	20	12.26
3 to 4 years' service	33	20.24
5 to 6 years' service	32	19.63
7 to 8 years' service	25	15.33
8 to 9 years' service	13	7.97
10 to 11 years' service	13	7.97
Above 11 years' service	22	13.49
Total	163	

The data in the above tables together indicate that the employment of women in rural areas is a new phenomenon.

The new role is bound to create problems of adjustment for the women employee. It is always easier for a person to play the institutionalised role, "In the stabilised pattern of interactions it becomes easy for the actor to adjust his conduct to some extent in order to meet with the other's expectations. The existing normative system, shared beliefs and criteria of evaluation and values which rank goals hierarchically in the institutionalised role, make it safer for the actor to play the institutionalised or traditional role in accordance with the expectations of the others." Especially, "In a high degree of institutionalisation of the role, a little in the performance or definition of the role is left to chance or to individual or collective interpretations." In such a case there is a lesser possibility of exposing the actor to the ambivalent motivation in the role performance.

The obverse of this also seems to be true. If the role is entirely new, the actor as well as alter are confused over the expectations from each other, 'The absence of such factors as, definite criteria of evaluation and values which rank goals hierarchically, shared beliefs and attitudes, clear-cut normative patterns etc. make it difficult for the actor to adhere to some definite behaviour pattern.' Many things are left to chance or to individual or collective interpretation. The actor is thus exposed to an unstructured situation. Here the element of ambivalence is introduced in the motivation of the actor. This ambivalence is bound to give rise to strain and frustration.

In the present context, woman's traditional roles as housewife and mother are more or less institutionalised. In India, girls are trained and socialised from the early childhood, for these roles. The woman is aware of her adult roles from an early age. So, there is little ambiguity in playing these roles. But the new occupational role is bound to create confusion and ambivalence in the motivational structure of the employed woman, for different reasons. Firstly, as the employment of woman is a recent phenomenon, she is not socialised for this role in her childhood. Secondly, even today the role of Wage earner outside the home is always considered as the male role in Indian society. So, here she is confused, whether she should be more committed to traditional sex role norms or to the emergent norms of her occupational role. Thirdly, as the role is a new one, the criteria of evaluation, shared beliefs and attitudes, distinct norms, values etc. are yet to evolve. So, many things are left to chance or to the individual or collective interpretation, bringing in an element of confusion in the interaction.

That the new role exposes the actor to the insecurities and uncertainties is clear from the following illustration too, "As a rule, it is easier to adjust one's behaviour to signals from other's conduct than to discern on one's own account, the relevant signals in a complicated environment. Miller and Dallard illustrate this point with the following examples... It is easier to drive behind the vehicle of a friend to find the right way in a strange city than to find for oneself even with the aid of maps."[3]

The following responses from the respondents reveal the presence of ambivalence in their minds about the right conduct. One Gramsevika said, "Many times, we have to accompany the officers on tour, sitting beside them in the same vehicle. If we sit beside them in the jeep, we are criticised for going too nearer to the male officers, neglecting the norm of keeping oneself away from men and having no scruples of behaviour befitting a modest women. If we avoid going along with the officers, the officers feel that we are avoiding our duty. In such a situation, what to do is a big problem for us. One teacher respondent said, "On many occasions, due to the exigencies of the work, we are required to stay long hours in the school. But if we stay for long hours in the school as our male colleagues do, it is not liked by our family members nor by the people in the village. If we neglect the work in the school, it would probably lead to frictions with the higher authority. It becomes then problematic for us to decide whether to stay at the school for long hours or return home."

Dr. Taylor rightly points out how difficult it becomes for one to cope with the new situation, "New ways of doing and thinking, always create ethical and spiritual insecurities. Change automatically creates uncertainty about what is really happening and what can be expected. Furthermore, old ways practised for generations are likely to be considered as sacred."[4]

From the above discussion it is clear that it becomes difficult for the individual to play a new role because of absence of any stabilised pattern of mutual expectations. This exposure to the new role is, thus, a problem faced by the employed woman in rural areas.

Incapabilities

The successful handling of any occupational role requires the occupant of the occupational position to have requisite qualifications, formal as well as informal along with other qualities. If the occupant is not equipped with these qualifications, it becomes difficult for him to play his occupational role effectively.

The scope of Community Development Programme was extended to cover the womenfolk of the villages only after 1952.

This necessitated the recruitment of women workers for carrying out the developmental schemes. But in the initial period, the dearth of women workers having requisite qualifications was seriously felt for different reasons. One reason was that employment of woman was a new phenomenon. The second reason of this dearth was the general apathy and fear entertained by parents and guardians of the qualified girls to send them to remote villages. The third reason was that though the girls having requisite qualifications were available in sufficient number in cities, these girls themselves were not willing to go to the villages, setting aside the attraction for city life.

Due to this scarcity, it seems, that women with less than the necessary educational qualifications or without vocational training were also recruited to these posts. The discussions with the higher officers of CDP confirmed this point. The author discussed this point with such officers as Chief Executive Officer of Zilla Parishad, Block Development Officers, District Educational Officer and with many other officers connected with the developmental activities in rural areas. The officers stated that there was generally dearth of suitable women employees to work in rural areas. But while appointing women having less than the minimum required qualifications, it was thought that these women would be sent for training or for refresher's courses after their appointment and then they would be qualified for carrying out their respective duties. But to their disappointment, the officers added, that many of these women employees went on postponing their vocational training, once they were appointed.

It may not be impertinent here to Examine the nature of vocational training given to these women workers. The discussion with some women employees revealed that the vocational training imparted to them was generally in the nature of acquisition of technical skills in the particular profession e.g., auxiliary nurse midwives are trained in midwifery, human anatomy, physiology etc., Gramsevikas under the nutrition scheme are trained in preserving the nutrition propensities of food etc. (For the teachers, vocational training is not compulsory). But their training, it seems, does not include the general study of the social structure of the community. They need not have to study attitudes, belief patterns, values of the people amidst whom and for whom they have to work. If such training had been given to the employed woman, she would have been better equipped herself as an effective agent of the envisaged planned social change. S.C. Dube discusses the qualities required for an effective agent of change in the following paragraph, "Insight into the inner workings of the community alone can give him the instinct to make the right choice... Unless he has a firm grasp over the most effective media of communication, backed by the understanding of the symbols, themes and appeals suited to the cultural idiom of the community, it may be difficult for him to put across his ideas to the people... Thus, he requires an orientation not only in regard to general motivations for change in a particular community but also some penetrating insights into the latent and manifest aspects of its internal functioning."[5]

The following table reveals that most of the women (*i.e.* 70.5 precent) have educational qualifications below the matriculation level, 115 women out of 163 have passed the seventh standard only.

TABLE 12

Distribution of Women Employees According to their Educational Qualifications

Education	Number of Women	%
Less than the 7th standard	5	3.06
7th standard pass	115	70.55
Matric pass	35	21.47
Under-graduate	1	0.61
Graduate	5	3.06
Post-graduate	2	1.22
Total	163	

It is doubtful to say that these women employees having less than required qualifications and the inadequate vocational training can discharge effectively their responsibilities entrusted to them as agents of social change. The aim of the Community Development Programme is to bring about an integrated cultural change in the village life. As Dube says the aim of C.D. Programme is, "To initiate and direct a process of integrated cultural change aimed at transforming the social and economic life of the villages."[6] The programme is conceived to bring about revolutionary changes in the attitudes, ways of life and values of rural women. And these changes are to be brought about by imparting social education to the masses, and creating in them the needs of self development. So, the agents of change must have, not only some professional skill but must have knowledge of how to deal with the people on man to man level. Dr. Durganand Sinha puts it thus. "Regarding the role of the official concerned with the programme, it has been suggested that he must listen to the villagers understand and help them to formulate their needs...... This implies a kind of therapeutic role which the community development personnel is expected to perform."[7] It is doubtful whether a woman having very low educational qualifications would understand the basic aims of these development schemes and would perform her role in an expected manner.

One also needs to have certain typical personality traits for the proper performance of occupational role. It is suggested that, "The successful occupational role is based on performance, effectiveness, qualification, information, ability, independence and initiative."[8] Indian woman as she is socialized for housewife's role only lacks in these qualities which are essential for playing the occupational role effectively. Submission and resignation are pronounced in Hindu Woman's personality. As pointed out by Cormack (1953)...... "Hindu women are submissive and that they do not fulfil their potentialities or fully develop their individual personalities."[9] She further observes, "Woman is more a member of a group than an individual, initiative is not encouraged, and there is little place for it in the system. There is little social approval or encouragement of ambition of new ventures of deviant behaviour......

The general result is a compliant personality, and no other general type of personality could normally develop under such social conditions."[10] With these personality traits it naturally becomes difficult for her to play the occupational role. The occupational role demands self-enhancement while the Indian woman is trained for self-negation. As Nimcoff says, "Acceptance of the goals of marriage and work simultaneously may mean conflict for many, if not for all educated women and it inevitably presents difficulties. The problem is likely to become more acute and accentuated because fulfilment of the two goals requires qualities of different type. The attainment of goals of marriage requires 'self negation' and co-operation, while to be successful in the other pursuit requires self-enhancement and competition."[11] Bowman too says, "such integration of the various elements of employed women's personality as may enable her to become adjusted to both situations, certainly presents a problem and the demands made by the two situations not only add to her worry and fatigue but may become a problem in itself."[12]

The other problem which was noted by the author in connection with these women employees was that they were not enough acquainted with the official procedures and formalities e.g., interpreting and drafting official letters, writing down the information and reports in the register or diary, application for pay bills or leave etc. Many respondents said, that they do not know all these matters and so, many times the male colleagues whose help they seek, exploit them for these things. There is very little opportunity for women to have informal training which would help them to adjust themselves to the male work world. Hence, they are rarely able to do their job independently. Often they are required to take the help of their male colleagues, who with the same length of service know many more things than they, in the office word.

This incompetence to handle the official procedures creates difficulties for women workers is obvious from the following narration of an officer. A Deputy Educational Inspector said, "Women are not at all conversant with the official routines such as writing and interpreting the official letters, applying for pay bills or leave etc. So they take the help of male colleagues. If the people in the office see that the man is helping the woman they suspect 'something' going on in between them. The pair, then becomes a subject of teasing and gossiping".

Thus, the low educational qualifications, combined with no tradition of working outside and non-acquaintance with the complex official procedures compel these women to depend upon their male-colleagues or officers for their help in these matters. In India, mixing with men is a taboo, "It was considered derogatory for a woman to take work outside the home, being primarily a question of social prestige and secondarily of involvement in the company of men."[13] Caught between inadequacy on one hand and pressure of social norms on the other, the woman suffers. Barbara Ward (1963) alludes to the same fact "In countries, where the seclusion of women has been traditional, life is often exceedingly difficult for those few women who have merged into the man's world....An Indian or Pakistani woman may find this same situation for more difficult, the separation of the sexes have been traditionally so marked that there may, at the out-set, appear to be virtually no respectable social pattern available for her and her male colleague to model their professional relationship upon."[14]

Thus incapability in managing the occupational role thus creates problems for working woman is obvious from the above discussion. This point can be confirmed by studying the following illustration, too, "Even though, the organization is stable and the role clear, the worker who does not have the capacity to fulfil his assignment is likely to have trouble. He may rebel against the job but he may also develop all sorts of devices for dealing with his inadequacies. These may encompass psychosomatic illness of fanciful worries......During World War II, the normal problem of employment appeared in exaggerated form, as number of people were thrust into jobs for which they had no preparation. Mrs. Strong talks of the foreman of a trucking crew who was effective until he was required to make written reports. Thereupon, he took to drink, became sullen and threatened his superiors with a knife. He could not write."[15]

The lack of requisite qualifications, formal as well as informal, has thus the stumbling block in the path of women employees for effective performance of their occupational role.

Woman Employee and Her Superiors

The occupational world is new to the Indian woman. In addition to that, she has double responsibilities of home and work.. So, sympathetic considerations by her superiors would create favourable atmosphere for the woman to play her role properly as an employee.

During the British rule, the relations between the officer and his subordinate were governed by superior-subordinate mentality even in social matters. It was significant to know whether any change has taken place in the nature of relationship between the members of different layers of bureaucracy after Independence. It was essential so, because the developmental programmes which were undertaken required spirited team workers for their proper implementation. Moreover, it was equally essential to know how the officers behave with these women employees. So, the inquiry was carried out in the present study about the behaviour patterns of officers with the women employees.

The following table indicates that 102 out of 163 women employees openly admitted that they are treated as inferiors by their officers. In the informal discussions with the employees, it was revealed that even petty officers always show off their superior positions.

TABLE 13

Low Status Accorded to Women Employees by the Officers

Response	Number of Women	%
Yes	102	62.57
No	61	37.42
Total	163	

The fact was verified by consulting a number of officers by the author. Though the officers said that they usually give considerate treatment to the women employees, they were unanimous in their opinion about the incompetence of the women employees. The officers expressed their sense of complete dissatisfaction regarding the performance of these women. They said that it was a sheer waste of money to employ these women. They have neither the ability nor any urge to do the official work properly. They said that they were more interested in their home affairs. Officer's attitude can be interpreted in the following way, "It seems clear that traditional thinking on the labour market, like discrimination of any kind, is essentially what Sociologists term a self-fulfilling prophecy. Women are regarded as less reliable workers in many sectors and treated accordingly. This treatment results in less efficiency on the average in the work in question, which in turn, gives further confirmation of traditional views."[16]

That even in the developed countries, the traditional sex role becomes a handicap for women in occupational field is amply seen in the following mentioned studies, "That the sex role is a handicap for women in working life has been illustrated by industrial sociological studies in Norway, Sweden and England, of the attitudes of male co-workers and superiors. The attitudes found can be summerised as follows: Women lack stability in working life. They do not feel identified with their job. They are unconcerned with the difficulties, such an attitude creates for co-workers and supervisors. They lack deep interest in their job and training."[17]

"Women win personal esteem by being feminine and men by being masculine. According to the traditional sex role norms, women should be weaker than men, require protection, be passive, patient, self-sacrificing, sensitive etc. *i.e.* possess qualities that cannot be regarded as qualifying them for the more important positions in industry or public life. Women win esteem by being women."[18]

As the concept of woman that she is fit for her sex role only is fixed in the minds of people, her work-role outside becomes a problem for her. It is clear from the above studies that she is evaluated from a prejudiced point of view.

Many respondents told the author that on many occasions, the officers put them to humiliation. The respondents made some difference between male officers and female officers. It was a surprise to know, from the respondents that the male superiors behave better with them than the female superiors. According to the respondents, male bosses are somewhat more considerate than female ones. Does this reflect the traditional superiority of man which is accepted by the Indian woman ? In India the traditional pattern of relationship between man and woman is of superiority and inferiority type. From the early childhood women are socialised to accept this. So, women employees might be willing to accept the superiority of men officers but at the same time they might be resenting the superiority of female bosses.

The author too, witnessed on many occasions, incidents of humiliation of these women employees at the hands of her superiors. One incident would bring this point in the proper perspective.

Once the author visited a village, 16 kms. from Parbhani town for the purpose of interviews of women employees in that village. The author was accompanied by some women office bearers. They camped in the village school. There, the Gramsevika working in that village was summoned. The Vice-President asked her, in the presence of others and in a very arrogant manner why she had not yet started the Balwadi (a school for small children) and why she didn't go to Parbhani to bring the utensils and the other material required for running the Balwadi. She said that as the Sirpanch (Village Head) of the village was not making proper arrangement for the accommodation of Balwadi, inspite of her several efforts, she was not able to do any progress. She further said that as she was not well she did not go to Parbhani, to collect the necessary material from the office. She added that on the day when she arrived in the village, she could not get proper accommodation, and had to take shelter in the veranda of the Gram Panchayat (office of the village head). So, she got cold and cough. Then, one of the office bearers present there reprimanded, "You are a first-rate liar. You don't want to do your duty. You will realise your arrogance only when your pay will be cut."

Afterwards the author tried to take her interview in a closed room. The woman employee was so down with the humiliation meted to her by the authority that she started sobbing. In a sobbing tone she said, "Now I am not able to say anything. I will come to your house and will narrate you everything." While on the return journey from the village, the officials told the author, "This woman employee is a spinster. She is not knowing even the usual etiquettes of behaviour. She never stands before the superior officers as a mark of respect. She directly approaches the higher authorities. So, we wanted to teach her a lesson. We will cut her pay, then only she will realise."

This incident shows how the authorities usually behave with the employees. On many occasions the author witnessed the show of authority and power by the officers in the presence of these employees. Such a treatment is bound to affect the role performance of the employees, negatively. This is illustrated by Dube (1960). He observes, "Treatment such as this in which the V.L.W. is dealt with as a subordinate of low status and no consequence frustrated the man in the field and kills his zeal for work. It is essential to curb the 'boss mentality' so that a healthy team spirit may be created."[19]

The following table illustrates the behaviour patterns of officers in relation to these employees in detail.

TABLE 14

Behaviour Patterns of Officers with the Women Employees

Response	Number of Women	%
Sympathetically	65	39.87
Casually	42	25.76
Derogatory	56	34.35
Total	163	

The data in the above table indicates that 56 (34.35 percent) respondents complained about the contemptuous behaviour patterns of the officers towards them. The data were further cross tabulated. It was analysed to ascertain the relationship between the variables such as caste, age, education etc. and the scornful treatment by the officers.

TABLE 15
Behaviour Pattern of Officers and the Nature of Service of the Women Employees

Nature of Service	Sympathetic	Casual	Scornful	Total
Nurse	13 (22.8%)	24 (42.1%)	20 (35.1%)	57
Teacher	40 (64.5%)	10 (16.1%)	12 (19.3%)	62
Gramsevika	12 (27.3%)	8 (18.1%)	24 (54.6%)	44
Total	65	42	56	163

TABLE 16
Behaviour Pattern of Officers and the Caste of the Women Employees

Caste	Sympathetic	Casual	Scornful	Total
Brahmin	26 (45.6%)	14 (24.5%)	17 (29.8%)	57
Middle Castes	20 (30.8%)	15 (23.1%)	30 (46.1%)	65
Lower Castes	6 (31.5%)	7 (37 %)	6 (31.5%)	19
Other Religions	13 (59 %)	6 (27.3%)	3 (13,6%)	22
Total	65	42	56	163

TABLE 17
Behaviour Pattern of Officers and Marital Status of the Women Employees

Marital Status	Sympathetic	Casual	Scornful	Total
Un-Married	5 (31.2%)	6 (37.6%)	5 (31.2%)	16
Married	48 (44.1%)	26 (23.8%)	35 (32.1%)	109
Widow	7 (31.9%)	6 (27.2%)	9 (40.9%)	22
Separated	5 (31.2%)	4 (25 %)	7 (43.8%)	16
Total	65	42	56	163

TABLE 18
Behaviour Pattern of Officers and Age-group Distribution of the Women Employees

Age group	Sympathetic	Casual	Scornful	Total
18-20 yrs.	—	4 (100%)	—	4
21-25 yrs.	24 (45.3%)	10 (18.8%)	19 (35.9%)	53
26-30 yrs.	16 (35.5%)	17 (37.8%)	12 (26.7%)	45
31-35 yrs.	12 (44.5%)	6 (22.2%)	9 (33.3%)	27
36-40 yrs.	6 (35.3%)	2 (11.8%)	9 (52.9%)	17
Above 40	7 (41.1%)	3 (17.8%)	7 (41.1%)	17
Total	65	42	56	163

TABLE 19
Behaviour Pattern of Officers and Education level of the Women Employees

Education	Sympathetic	Casual	Scornful	Total
Less than 7th Standard	2 (40 %)	1 (20 %)	2 (40 %)	5
7th Standard Pass	46 (40 %)	29 (25.2%)	40 (34.8%)	115
Matric Pass	13 (35.1%)	10 (28.6%)	12 (34.3%)	35
Under Graduate	1 (100%)	—	—	1
Graduate	3 (60 %)	1 (20 %)	1 (20 %)	5
Post-Graduate	—	1 (50 %)	1 (50 %)	2
Total	65	42	56	163

The data in the preceding Tables 15 to 19 reveal the following points:

1. The data in the Table 15 shows that the Gramsevikas and nurses on the whole are treated more scornfully than the teachers, by the officers. It suggests connection between the type of service of the employee and possibility of her being treated scornfully by the officers. Teaching profession wields more prestige in society than the other two and that explains why the teachers are treated more sympathetically. (The point is dealt with, at length later).
2. Table 16 indicates that the caste of the employee as a factor has a relevance for the scornful treatment which she gets at the hands of her superiors. The data show that the women employees belonging to the Higher

castes are treated more sympathetically than those of middle castes and lowest castes.

(3) The data in the Table 17 show that widows and separated women employees are treated more scornfully than married and unmarried women employees. In India, marriage only confers status on women. So, this might be the reason why widows and separated women get contemptuous treatment at the hands of the officers.

(4) Table 18 draws attention to the fact that the percentage of scornful treatment, by the officers to the women employees belonging to age group 36-40, is higher than that to the women employees belonging to other age-groups.

(5) The study of the Table 19 denotes that there exists correlation between the educational level of women employees and the scornful treatment to them by the officers. The data show that the women employees who are educated below the level of matriculation are treated in a more derogatory way than those having higher educational qualifications.

Molestation

We often hear of frightful and shocking incidents of molestation of women employees in the villages. It was obvious from the reports of the incidents that not only hooligans and the leaders but even the officers also were involved in molesting the women employees. So, a question was included in the schedule to test the validity of these complaints. At the outset, it was presumed that women would not openly admit of attempt of molestation on their modesty by the officers, as they would think that such an admission would endanger their moral character. So, another question was included in the schedule to ascertain whether they know any cases of harassment or molestation of other women employees. The data thus collected are given here.

TABLE 20

Molestation of Women Employees by the Officers

Response	Number of Women employees	%
Yes	18	11.04
No	145	88.95
Total	163	

TABLE 21

Molestation by the Officers and the Nature of Service of the Women Employees

Nature of Service	Molested (Yes)	Total
Nurse	7 (12.2%)	57
Teacher	4 (6.4%)	62
Gramsevika	7 (15.9%)	44
Total	18	163

TABLE 22

Molestation by the Officers and the Caste of the Women Employees

Caste	Molested (Yes)	Total
Brahmins	8 (14.0%)	57
Middle Castes	7 (10.7%)	65
Lower Castes	1 (5.2%)	19
Other religions	2 (9.0%)	22
Total	18	163

TABLE 23
Molestation by the Officers and the Marital Status of the Women Employees

Marital Status	Molested (Yes)	Total
Unmarried	4 (25%)	16
Married	11 (10%)	109
Widow	1 (4%)	22
Separated	2 (12%)	16
Total	18	163

TABLE 24
Molestation by the Officers and Age-group of Women Employees

Age-group	Molested (Yes)	Total
18-20 yrs.	—	4
21-25 yrs.	7 (13.2%)	53
26-30 yrs.	4 (8.8%)	45
31-35 yrs.	2 (7.4%)	27
36-40 yrs.	2 (11.1%)	17
Above 40	3 (17.6%)	17
Total	18	163

TABLE 25
Molestation by the Officers and Education level of the Women Employees

Education	Molested (Yes)	Total
Less than 7th stdndard	1 (20%)	5
7th Standard Pass	13 (11.3%)	115
Matric Pass	2 (5.7%)	35
Under Graduate	Nil (0%)	1
Graduate	1 (20%)	5
Post Graduate	1 (50%)	2
Total	18	163

The number of cases of molestation of women employees is too small to analyse, still an attempt is made to find out the social variables involved in molestation cases. As the date in the above tables reveal, that there exists no significant relationship between caste, marital status, age and education of the women employees and their molestation. From Table 21 it seems there exists some relationship between the nature of service of the employee and the incidence of her molestation.

Even though the number of respondents who were molested is very small yet, the above table indicates that considerable number of women employees know of the cases of molestation of their colleagues by the officers. This indicates that the reports about molestation of woman employees are not baseless. There must be many more incidents of molestation of these employees than are known to the people.

TABLE 26
"Do You Know any Cases of Molestation of Women Employees ?"

Response	Number of women employees	%
Yes	73	44.78
No	90	55.21
Total	163	

Problem of Transfers

"The main intention in making transfers is to prevent officials from creating vested interest for themselves and the tendency is likely to grow if they are allowed to continue at a place for a very long time. Transfers are made with a view to avoiding this danger and this principle is made applicable to the women employees also."[20]

This principle sounds good. But the other considerations involved in the matter of transfers should also command our attention. Many undesirable practices have crept into the transfer matters. This is clearly seen from the following tables.

Although, the principle behind transfers is to prevent the employees from creating vested interest for themselves, the above tables reveal, how foul practices are at work in transfer matters. 123 out of 163 (75.4 percent) of the women employees said that the transfers are not based on fair play. That such factors as revengeful attitude of the officers, pressure from the leaders, convenience of more influential employees etc. are always playing their part in transfer matters, is clearly evident in the above tables. Almost all respondents have admitted that graft and pressure of influential people are the catchwords in transfer matters, "Lach (Bribe) ani vashilaya shivay Badali Nahi." All the respondents suggested that bribing an influential leader, does good in transfer matters. One respondent said,

TABLE 27
Factors behind Transfer

Factors	Number of Respondents	%
Departmental convenience	28	17.17
Revengeful attitude of officers	7	4.29
Complaints by villagers	8	4.90
Pressure from Leaders	9	5.52
To make room for influential employees	12	7.36
All the above reasons	87	53.37
No knowledge of factors behind transfer	12	7.36
Total	163	100

TABLE 28
The Means Adopted by Employees for Transfers

Means adopted	Number of Employees	%
Personal request	32	19.63
Pressure through leaders	24	14.72
Presents and Bribes	3	1.84
All the above reasons	98	60.12
Through application	2	1.22
None of these means adopted	1	0.61
No knowledge of these means	3	1.84
Total	163	

Road side places and villages near by cities are always in demand. So the employees have to bribe the local leaders or influential persons to get them transferred to these places or retain themselves at these places. One respondent said, "There are several examples of employees who, by seeking the favour of influential leaders, are sticking to such convenient places for twelve to fifteen years. They are never transferred."

The author too, had noted one incident of such kind. One teacher was transferred to Parbhani town through the favour of one of the influential leaders. The teacher herself admitted that she has been at Parbhani for the last ten years.

The respondents told that the leaders demand something in return of their favour. They not only demand bribe but exploit these employees for their personal benefits. They use them in election compaigns or these employees, sometimes, are asked to do such humiliating jobs such as serving food in marriage feasts or in other private functions. One teacher respondent admitted, "Through the influence of a leader I was transferred to the place which I desired. But in return, I have to take tuitions of the children of the leader free of cost. If I reject to do that, I will be transferred to some distant place immediately."

Another complaint which was often heard from the respondents was that long distance transfers are often effected, e.g. employees are transferred from Nagpur to Parbhani, Thana to Parbhani, from Kolhapur to Parbhani etc. In the present inquiry there were many incidents of long distance transfers.

The transfer dislocates family life of the woman employee, specially of the married one. They are confronted with the problems of the education of children, of maintaining households at two places, of adjustment to the new situation and the like.

The respondents expressed their reactions regarding the long distance transfers in the following way, "Generally women are not ready to go to a far away places. So, villagers when they see us coming from far away place all along leaving our family, they are suspicious about us." There is sharp competition for the job these days because of acute problem of unemployment. These new jobs have given these women employees warmth of economic security which they fear they would lose in case they complain against anything connected with the employment including transfers.

It is through the mechanism of transfer that some of the officers exercise their dominant power over the employees and can constrain them to yield. All the villages in the district are not equally well situated. Some of them are well connected with cities or towns by good roads and some are not. Some have better medical, educational, transport facilities than others. The employees, especially the woman employees always cherish to be transferred to the better situated places and for this they have to carry favour with officers, the non-officials or influential leaders. This they can do by employing various means such as by doing petty jobs for them, by offering presents to them, by showing extravagant hospitality to them or helping the leaders in their election campaigns etc. Graft in hidden or open form is not barred. It is rumoured that the amounts of grafts reach these persons through their agents and transfers are thereon effected. Transfers are also used as mechanism of punishment. Those, who are not in the good books of their superiors are often punished by transfers to remote, inconvenient villages. One scheduled caste teacher narrated the injustice done to her in the following words, "My husband and I both work as teachers. There is a rule that both husband and wife should be transferred to the same places. But for the last ten years we have been at different places. Inspite of our several requests the things have remained unchanged. We are not fortunate enough to have influential contracts. So, we have to accept it as our fate. If we complain about it to the higher authorities, we fear that revenge would be taken on us."

It was clearly perceived that sheer monitary gains are pushing these women to work in villages. So, whatever may be the injustices meted to them, these employees try to swallow them. They don't want to verbalise them by complaining against them. The author often sensed this fear in the minds of these employees.

Promotions

Promotion is one of the social mechanism which induces one to work hard and be efficient in playing one's occupational role. The lure of promotion often draws out efficient performance capacity of the actor in a situation. But the data in the following table clearly points out the blatant fact that very negligible number of employees could get promotions. Further inquiry has revealed that there are very few promotions left open to the employees of these occupational categories, 142 (87.11 percent) out of 163 women said that there are no promotions in their jobs. Lack of incentives of any kind in the occupation may be regarded as a factor responsible for indifferent attitude of these employees towards their occupational role.

TABLE 29
Promotion Possibilities

Response	Number of Women Employees responded	%
Received promotion	15	9.20
Could not get promotion	142	87.11
No promotion offered in the service	6	3.68
Total	163	

No Protection from Trade Unions

The data in the following table show the working of trade unions among these employees, 98 out of 163 women said that they are not members of any trade union protecting the rights of the employees. 65 women said that though they belong to some or other workers' unions of general type. These unions are not meant exclusively for protecting the interests of women employees. So it seems, the unions to which some of the women employees belong, tackle the general problems of the employees as such and not the particular problems of women employees, e.g., Maharashtra Rajya Zilla Parishad Karmachari Union, Gramsevak Union etc.

TABLE 30
Are you a Member of any Trade Union Organisation ?

Response	Number of Women	%
Yes	65	39.87
No	44	26.99
Not aware of any such organization	54	33.12
Total	163	

From the data it is clear that there are no united efforts made on the part of women employees in rural areas to agitate for the solution of their problems. They seem to be shy of active trade unionism. The reason might be as stated by Padmini Sengupta that, "There is a general apathy on the part of women towards trade unions, though the part they are playing in strikes and agitations is increasing. The main reason for non-participation of women in trade unionism is the pull of religion and traditional social customs. A woman worker also has countless domestic chores to attend to, after her work which leaves little time for other activities."[21]

It is heartening to note that very recently the Maharashtra State Government Employees Nurses Association has strongly protested against the insecurity of the nurses in villages. The Maharashtra State Government Employees Nurses Association has threatened to launch a statewide agitation if the Government fails to provide security for the nurses in villages.

Tours

As a part of their duty, women employees of certain categories have to undertake tours. Touring is a pre-requisite for the posts of Gramsevikas, Nurses, Mid-wives, female field workers etc. The following table indicates the number of women employees who have to undertake tours.

TABLE 31
Tours

Response	Number of women employees	%
Have to undertake tours	90	55.21
No tours	73	44.98
Total	163	

It was noticed that almost all respondents who have to take tours, were very unhappy with this part of their duty. They cited various difficulties which they have to face on this count. One respondent said, "On many occasions we have to accompany the officers or other non-officials on tour in the same vehicle. We have to sit nearby them. Sometimes men sitting near us start taking undue liberaties with us. We cannot complain about it as they are our superiors and secondly we are afraid of possible stigma which will be stamped on our character." Another respondent said, "As we accompany the male officers on tours in the same jeep, villagers are suspicious about us." Another respondent cited other difficulties. She said, "Sometimes we have to cover small distances of two to three miles on foot while touring the nearby villages. We often meet goondas on our way. They start teasing us in any immodest way." Especially, nurses and female field workers of family planning programme said that it is very difficult for them to undertake tours due to the menace of goondas. Many respondents cited that the nuisance of drunkards in villages is also not negligible. They said that they have to face danger from wild animals, snakes, thieves etc., too.

In India, the respectable pattern for women for going out is that they should be accompanied by family members. Seldom they go all alone outside. So women going all alone on tours are, judged by the villagers, goondas, officers, leader's etc. from a different angle. A woman employee accepting a touring job is conveniently regarded by the villagers as one having no scruples about modest behaviour befitting a good woman. And it seems, there the nuisance starts.

Job-satisfaction

"Job-satisfaction is an important element affecting the role performance of the actor. The more one is satisfied with the job, the more one is likely to exert oneself to play the role effectively. But if one is not satisfied with the role which one is playing, mechanical implementation of the rudimentary requisites of the role is likely to take place. The actor is likely to cling to the safe routines of the role rather than the spirit of it. This is also a kind of deviance from the ideal conformity to the role."

The following two tables clearly reveal the element of dissatisfaction prevalent among these employees about their jobs in the village.

TABLE 32

"Will You Leave the Present Job for a Job in the City ?"

Response	Number of women employees	%
Yes	134	82.20
No	29	17.79
Total	163	

TABLE 33
"Do You feel like Leaving this Service ?"

Response	Number of women employees	%
Yes	101	61.96
No	62	38.03
Total	163	

The inspection of the above table shows that a considerable number of women are not satisfied with their job.

The amount of satisfaction one gets out of one's job depends upon several factors such as economic, esthetic and symbolic rewards attached to the job, clear stable, non-ambiguous and meaningful role, feeling of security ; one's ability in handling the role effectively etc. Let us scrutinize their role in the context of these factors.

On the basis of the data collected, it can be said that the economic rewards, which these posts carry are more or less proportionate to the need dispositions of these employees.

The following table roughly indicates this. 95 out of 163 women employees *i.e.* more than 50 percent, said that they are satisfied with the economic rewards of their job.

TABLE 34
Are You Satisfied with Your Pay ?

Response	Number of women employees	%
Yes	95	58.28
No	68	41.71
Total	163	

Does their role carry any esthetic rewards ? Many respondents said that they did not feel any charm in their job. Village life is dull and without excitement and entertainment. Many employees complained that the villagers do not give proper response to the work which they do for them. Though the statistical data was not gathered on the esthetic rewards of the job, the total impression which the author gathered was that these employees get little esthetic rewards from their job.

Are there any symbolic rewards ? The following words of these employees indicate that the job carries little symbolic rewards. One Gramsevika said, "I feel humiliated to tell people that I am working as a Gramsevika in village." One Nurse gave vent to her feelings about her job in the following manner, "Sometimes it becomes difficult for us to get accommodation in the village as a neighbour of a respectable family due to our profession. This is the way people look at our profession." One teacher said, "In the village, in modern time people who have political power enjoy prestige. Teacher's profession is not held in esteem as it was before. Women teachers are called 'Dhanagarin' " (Shephardess, the word used for denoting low status, by the villagers).

The above expressions reveal that these women are conscious of the low status accorded to them. They are aware that their employment carries little prestige, esteem and power.

It seems that the nature of the role too, is responsible for creating dissatisfaction among the large number of employees.

In the present inquiry, the tabulated data on job-satisfaction was further analysed to see whether such factors as age, marital status, caste, having young children etc. have any relevance for employees' job-satisfaction. But after careful scrutiny it was found that no significant relationship exists between these variables and the job-satisfaction. But it was seen that there exists correlation between job-satisfaction of the employee and the nature of her service.

The above table discloses that Nurses are the most dissatisfied among the women employees. The reasons seem to be the role of the Nurse is not clearcut and multiservice demands are made on her. The following rough job-chart of the Nurse would prove this.

TABLE 35

Job Satisfaction and the Nature of Service

Nature of Service	Not satisfied	Total
Nurses	41 (71.9%)	57
Teachers	22 (35.4%)	62
Gramsevikas	28 (63%)	44

Job-chart of the Nurse

1. General care of the health of mother and child.
2. Pre-natal and post-natal care of the mother.
3. Attending to the delivery calls.
4. Propagation of family planning methods among men as well as women.
5. Persuading people for their sterilization and then taking them to the nearby hospitals for operations. Attending on these patients after operation.
6. Touring nearby villages.
7. Treating the sick patients.
8. Administering public health measures such as small-pox vaccination, cholera inoculations etc.
9. Writing diary, keeping the record of distribution of family planning devices, keeping the record of births and deaths.
10. Attending monthly meetings and other health camps etc. The nurse has to take tours in the morning and attend the dispensary in the afternoon.

This is a complicated work scheduled for a nurse. Damle in his study of A.N.M. points out that the consequences of such role in the following words, "In field situations, demands for omnibus services are made on the A.N.M. In fact even according to the programme as envisaged by the state, the A.N.M. is loaded with many kinds of functions for which she is not equipped in terms of the training received by her. This situation is very likely to have consequences for the programme, the personnel and the community."[22]

The job-chart of the nurse shows that her role demands multi-services from her and also it is not so well defined. The discussion on 'inabilities' in the present chapter has revealed that most of the women are not equipped properly, formally as well as informally to handle their role, effectively. An analysis of the few cases of molestation of women employees reveal that nurses and gramsevikas are more insecure than teachers. So, from the above discussion we can deduce that the ambiguous nature of the role, inadequate training resulting in many inabilities, sense of insecurity etc. are also the factors responsible for the sense of dissatisfaction which these nurses have about their job.

The role of Gramsevika too, is ambiguous in nature. Her job-chart includes the following things :

1. Visiting five houses daily and persuading women to keep their children clean and neat, telling them to keep their houses clean and airy.
2. To teach the women folk of the villages to grow kitchen gardens, to start poultry-farms etc.
3. To teach the village women folk, the modern methods of preserving grains, vegetables etc.
4. To teach the women embroidery, sewing and culinary art.
5. To promote teenagers associations, Balwadis, women's associations etc.
6. To propagate nutritious food schemes.
7. To arrange social education camps.
8. To organise listeners' groups for listening to the radio programmes.
9. To give publicity to the various Government schemes for the villagers such as Family Planning etc.

10. To write office-diary and keep record of the materials brought and used for the sake of various schemes.

The analysis of the above job-chart shows that the Gramsevika has to play the role of an innovator in the village. The overall nature of her role seems to be of a social educator. Her role involves persuasion of women of the villages to accept the new ways. The gist of her role consists in bringing about changes in the attitudes of the women in villages. Therefore, it is very difficult to measure or evaluate her role performance. The element of ambiguity in her role might be creating dissatisfaction in her mind about her job.

Clearcut and stable role brings efficiency in the role playing. As Spaulding Charles observes, "to be effective, the worker needs to have a clear and stable role and task. For some years the great emphasis on the work group and the human aspect of the job tended to cause some lack of emphasis upon these important factors of clarity and stability. But the necessity for them flows clearly from the basic conception of what social organization really is, for it, people are to work together successfully, a considerable amount of precision must inhere in the role assigned to each. Several pieces of research have tended to re-emphasize this aspect of the productive job."[23] Like Nurses, the Gramsevikas too have to handle ambiguous role, they are also victims of inability in many matters connected with their job. They also harbour insecurity due to the reported cases of molestation. They themselves do not find any meaningfulness in their role. Damle in his study of A.N.M. gives a note of warning in this respect, "It is not necessary to labour the point how very vital it is, that the programme must be meaningful to those who implement it. Otherwise there would be either mechanical implementation of the programme or at worst a complete lack of co-operation in its implementation. The factor of deceitful practices arising out of this situation, cannot be left out of account."[24]

Compared with the role of Nurse and Gramsevika, the role of the teacher is somewhat clear-cut and stable. It enjoys some prestige and security. So, teachers seem to be more satisfied with their work.

The above discussion shows that the roles of these employees, in general, carry little esthetic or symbolic rewards. Their roles are ambiguous in nature and carry little meaning even to themselves. Inabilities and sense of insecurity are also significant elements in the present context. So, all these factors can be viewed as factors contributing to the sense of dissatisfaction about the job for these employees.

Summary

For generations, Indian women have been trained for her roles within the family only. So the new occupational role is bound to create the problems of adjustment in both the fields. In this chapter an attempt was made to bring forth her problems in her occupational field.

An Exposure to a completely alien role, incapacities inherent in her personality to handle the occupational role, derogatory and non-sympathetic treatment accorded to her by the officers, absence of promotions, unfair deals in transfer matters, touring job etc. are some of her problems in this new field.

Can a genesis of her problems be explained by using Merton's status-set theory as used by Promilla Kapoor ? She says, "The occupational role of woman results in the extension of status-set of woman. Since each status has its accompanying role-set, this additional status adds another complement of a role-set. Members in a role-set put demands, sometimes conflicting, on the incumbent of status position. When person is involved in several role-sets by virtue of occupying different statuses, the demands made by different role-sets are more often than not incompatible and infeasible resulting in status conflict."

Or, can the genesis of her occupational problems be explained by using Parsons' dilemma of "pattern variables ?" It seems her problems in this respect have arisen due to the confrontation of values of two groups which are diametrically opposite of each other. Indian woman throughout her life, is confined to the small primary group of family. Family embodies the values of particularism, diffuseness, affectivity and quality, while the occupational structure rests on universalism, performance, affective neutrality and specificity. Some of her problems can be attributed to the clash between these two group values.

REFERENCES

1. Ross Aileen, "The Hindu Family in Its Urban Setting" (University Toronto Press, Bombay, 1967) p. 200.
2. *Ibid.*, p. 292.
3. Dahlstrom Edmund (Ed.), "The Changing Roles of Men and Women" (Gerald Duckworth and Co. Ltd., London, 1967) p. 45.
4. Dr. Taylor's quotation as mentioned by Durganand Sinha, in "Indian Villages in Transition" (Associated Publishing House, Delhi, 1969) p. 211.
5. Dube S.C., in "Kurukshetra" (A Symposium On Community Development in India) (Publication Division, Government of India, Delhi, 1961) p. 81.
6. Dube S.C., "India's Changing Villages" (Routledge and Kegan Paul Ltd., London, 1958) p. 8.
7. Sinha Durganand, "Indian Villages in Transition" (Associate Publishing House, New Delhi, 1969), p. 209.
8. Dahlstrom Edmund (Ed.), "The Changing Roles of Men & Women" (Gerald Duckworth & Co., Ltd., London, 1967), p. 47.
9. Cormack Margaret, "The Hindu Woman" (Bureau of Publications, Teachers College, Columbia University, New York, 1953).
10. *Ibid.*, pp. 199-200.
11. Quotation of Nimcoff as mentioned by Kapoor, Promilla in "Marriage and the Working Woman" (Vikas Pub. New Delhi, 1971), pp. 14-15.
12. *Ibid.*
13. Kapadia K.M., "Marriage and Family in India" (Oxford University Press, London, 1966), p. 263.
14. Ward Barbara E. (Ed.), "Women in New Asia" (UNESCO, Paris, 1963) p. 74.
15. Spaulding Charles, "An Introduction to Industrial Sociology" (D.B. Taraporevala Sons & Co. Private Ltd., Bombay 1970), p. 247.
16. Dahlstrom Edmund (Ed.), "The Changing Roles of Men and Women" (Gerald Duckworth and Co. Ltd., London, 1967), p. 187.

17. *Ibid*., p. 49.
18. *Ibid*., p. 190.
19. Dube S.C., "India's Changing Villages" (Routledge and Kegan Paul Ltd., London, 1960). Appendix II, p. 220.
20. "Problems facing Women Employees in Government Service" (Central Administration Deptt., Govt. of Maharashtra, Bombay, 1972), p. 27.
21. Sengupta, Padmini, "Women Workers of India" (Asia Publishing House, Bombay 1960), p. 68.
22. Damle, Y.B., "Auxiliary Nurse Mid-wife" (Deccan College, Poona 6), p. 240.
23. Spaulding, Charles B., "An Introduction to Industrial Sociology" (D.B. Taraporevala & Sons Co. Pvt. Ltd., Bombay 1970.) p. 244.
24. Damle, Y.B., "Auxiliary Nurse Mid-wife" (Deccan College, Poona 6), p. 260.

CHAPTER FIVE

EMPLOYED WOMAN AND THE RURAL COMMUNITY

THE PHENOMENON of employment of women in rural areas is of recent origin. Only after the Independence, different development schemes for the rural community were undertaken by the Government. This opened up wide opportunities for the women to secure gainful employment in rural areas. Specifically, the Community Development Programme and the Panchayati Raj offered scope to the women to work in villages.

Women from towns and cities were recruited for these jobs as women having adequate qualifications were not available from villages. This situation created several problems of adjustment for these employed women. Most of them had to leave the socio-cultural environment to which they were conditioned and set their foot in an unaccustomed one.

Another obvious point is that the nature of her role in the village, itself created problems of adjustment for her. All the developmental activities were planned changes, introduced in the rural community. The role of the employed woman was to act as an agent of these changes. The changes for the rural betterment were innovative in nature. Naturally, she has to play the role of an innovator.

Her role as an innovator suffered from certain limitations. She is not supposed to bring about innovations by coercive methods like her predecessors in the former bureaucratic set-up. But she has to coaxe the rural people, particularly the women-folk to accept the new ways of life. She is expected to study the felt needs of the people, as well to endeavour to create progressive needs in them. Instead of using coercive means, she has to function as a friend and a well-wisher and to a certain extent as a leader of the village women. She has to assist the women in rural areas to accept the scientific outlook, scientific techniques and many other new things in various fields. The overall nature of her role seems to be as an agent of modernization.

The nature of her role and the limitations on her role playing, created problems of adjustment for her. Because the social milieu of an Indian village was not ripe enough to welcome modernization. It is still struggling hard under the age-old traditional pattern of life. Mobility in different aspects of social life is the essence of modernization. But comparatively, immobility in different social fields was the key feature of the traditional Indian society. The employed woman was expected to bring about psychic mobility in certain aspects of the traditional social structure. But as Indian society was not very much prone to change, it tried to resist it. It can be appropriately explained in the words of Saksena in the following manner. "We clearly notice that the people of developing countries could not orient themselves in sufficient manner to confirm to social change process in a self-sustaining manner. Lerner stresses that these people wishing to better their lives, could not generate enough potentialities for psychic mobility to allow their old patterns and practices providing way to progressive elements of social change. People do want change but anchors of fatalistic ideas and traditional values are too heavy to be lifted up for sustained acquisition of novel and useful innovations characteristic of industrial societies."[1]

Innovations are always resisted, because they produce continual factors of change in the social system, "They disturb the established patterns of thinking and doing of the people. Stabilized patterns of life are always regarded as sacrosanct. The new ways are always suspected. People prefer "known benefits of a particular system to the unknown or doubtful benefits of change which may be feared in itself. People choose to maintain the status quo rather than the uncertainties of a particular type of change." Groups as well as individuals develop vested interests in the established patterns of life. So, due to the fear of possible threat to their interests, they resist change.

In the present context, the employed woman is bound to suffer from the problems of adjustment as she is new to her role, as well as, her role is new to the villagers.

In this chapter, an attempt is made to study her problems which arise due to the rural environment in which she has to work. Following are the problems investigated and analysed in the present chapter.

Harassment

In the recent years, we have been often hearing numerous stories of harassment of women employees in rural areas. The nature of tyranny to which she is subjected has gone to such an extent that sometimes, her very existence is at stake. The clippings from the newspapers included in an appendix to the thesis, amply demonstrate the manner in which these women are victimized. The cuttings cover the following cases :

1. A woman was working as a Family Planning worker in a village. Once, an attempt was made to rape her by some unknown miscreants. But it was reported that she rescued herself in a daring manner.
2. Another example is of a Gramsevika working in a village. One fine morning she was found burnt to death in her official quarter. Mystery hangs, whether it is a murder or a suicide.
3. The third case is also of a Gramsevika. It was reported that she was murdered by the villagers.
4. One trained Nurse was found dead in a hanged condition in her very small room in the village where she was working. Did she commit suicide ? One does not know.
5. Another example is of an unmarried Nurse. She was pregnant. Her officer who was said to be responsible for it, later on disowned his responsibility. In her attempt to abort herself she died.

6. One more case is of a Family Planning field worker. It was reported in the newspaper, that a local leader of the village where she was working, tried to rape her at night.
7. Another shocking example is of a mid-wife working in a village. This case was reported recently. One day, when she was returning home from her night duty, she was molested by village miscreants. The 'goondas' are reported to have torn her clothes completely in a bid to molest her.

These cases came to light because they got publicity in newspapers, discussed in Maharashtra State Assembly and was tried in law courts. But, many informants confided with the author and told that there were many other cases of such sort, lying hidden due to several reasons.

In Maharashtra State Assembly too, sometimes back, there was an uproar from opposition members about the pitiable plight of employed women in rural areas. The increase in the incidence of harassment of molestation of women employees in rural areas caused a wild commotion in the public and created widespread concern about the security of the women employees. The issue was hotly debated in the State Legislature. And finally, the result was that the Maharashtra Government appointed a state level committee to probe into the problems of women employees particularly of the women working in rural areas. The Committee has recommended certain measures for safeguarding the modesty of employed women in rural areas. This indicates the seriousness of the problem. So, in the present work questions were included in the schedule to find out the social variables involved in the problem of harassment.

The data about harassment were collected directly through the questionnaires as well as through personal discussions with many people. The analysis of the data shows that the harassment of these employees, is due to the interplay of various social variables. Family situation of the employee, her marital status, her caste and the nature of her service are the important determinants of her harassment. The data are tabulated here.

TABLE 36
Family Situation and Harassment of Women Employees

Members in the Family	No. of respondents harassed	Total
Living alone	28 (70%)	38
Living with husband	26 (50%)	51
Living with relatives	22 (58%)	38
Living with children only	29 (80%)	36
Total	85	163

The data in the above table clearly reveal that women living without husband or relatives are harassed more than those living with husband or relatives.

By tradition the role of woman in Indian society is mainly of wife and mother. Any new aspect of her role comes second. Seclusion of woman is a social value. It is regarded as a mark of prestige of the family. In modern times higher castes under the Western influence have granted more freedom to the women in social life. But, in the villages, the traditional value of confining women to the four walls of the home still dominates. In villages, only those women who belong to lower, economic and social strata, work outdoor. Women of higher castes are still confined to their families as a point of family prestige even in villages.

A general impression of many people is that woman working outdoor is accepted and approved in villages.* So, they think that there is no stigma attached to the employed woman as such. But the fact is that, even in villages, stigma is attached to the family of the working woman. Economically, she is presumed to be so badly off as her people are not in a

* Please see the introduction by B.N. Datar to "Women And Employment" S.N. Ranade & P. Ramchandran (Tata Institute of Social Science, Bombay, 1970), p. 1.

position to support her. Socially, it is regarded as indescent exposure of the woman of the family to the outsider. Women who work outside, in rural areas generally belong to very low economic and social strata. That, woman belonging to the middle class and employed outside home for economic remuneration, is something unusual to the tradition of Indian village. By tradition, woman is supposed to be economically dependant on man. So, the employed woman does not command that much esteem from the village people as the woman in the family commands.

Especially, in the Marathwada region where the present study was conducted, seclusion of woman is a mark of prestige for the family. Comparatively, Marathwada is an underdeveloped region in Maharashtra. Historically, as a part of the old Hyderabad State, Marathwada was under the domination of Muslim rule till 1956. So in social life we still witness the remnants of the Muslim culture. Among Muslims, women are put in Purdah (veil) as a mark of prestige. Due to the influence of Muslim culture, women belonging to the dominant caste and the higher castes confine themselves to the four walls of the home. So, in the context of this cultural background, employed woman, moving outside freely and living alone without the protection of husband or elderly persons is not favourably looked at.

The twin ideals about woman as exemplified by Dr. Alva Myrdal and Viola Klein in their brilliant analysis of 'Women's two roles' are prevalent even in Indian society. About Western societies they observe, "There is no use in denying that, even to-day, the twin-ideals of the hard working housewife and of the leisured lady exist in an (and as a rule unrecognized) alliance, jointly circumscribing woman's role as one to be acted out within the home."[2] Even in Indian society and especially in rural areas non-employed housewife enjoys more prestige than the employed one.

In Indian society, there are certain peculiar attitudes and beliefs about woman. Woman is regarded as weakling. So, all through her life she is protected by her male counterparts. Father, husband and son are supposed to be her protectors in the different stages of her life. Another notion about woman is that she is regarded as fickle, frail and faithless. So, she should always be guarded by men, "Through their passion for man, their unstable temper and inherent heartlessness they become disloyal to their husbands, however, carefully they may be guarded in this world." "A woman should never think of independence from the father, the husband or the sons because by so doing she will make both the families contemptible."[3] This concept of woman held by Hindu Shastrakaras is reflected in the attitude of the people towards women. The idea of independent individualistic western type of woman did not appear in Indian society. This situation makes the woman living alone more vulnerable to the harassment by the people.

Woman and her family are inseparable in India. Cormack points out this in following manner, "Women's sense of self, of power is usually developed within the family pattern. It must be realised there or not at all." So, woman living alone or with small children only is generally looked down upon.

In India, the qualities that women win the esteem are that she should be passive, patient, self-sacrificing and modest. But these qualities do not help the woman to cope up with the occupational world outside. Just the opposite qualities are needed to assert one's position in the occupational world. Women win esteem by playing the accepted feminine role of housewife and mother. Employed women display certain qualities which are necessary for occupational role playing and are regarded as unbecoming of a modest woman. This factor must be taken into the consideration with reference to the harassment of the women employees in the rural areas.

Many employed women have to live in villages either alone or without any elderly family member. This is due to a variety of reasons. But this situation is interpreted otherwise by the villagers as they are not used to see women living independently, without family protection. So it seems the attitude of the society, towards woman in the context of family, is responsible for her harassment.

(B) Marital Status and Harassment

The relation between marital status of the Woman employee and her harassment is quite evident from the data in the table given on page 94.

TABLE 37
Marital Status of the Women Employee and Harassment

Marital Status of employed women	No. of respondents harassed	Total
Unmarried	12 (75%)	16
Married	63 (57%)	109
Widow	16 (72%)	22
Separated	14 (87%)	16
Total	105	163

The percentage of harassed women is the highest among separated women. Unmarried girls and widows are more harassed than married women.

Why married women are less troubled than widows, separated or unmarried women, can be properly understood in the context of the social attitude of the Indian people towards marital status of woman.

Marriage is a social and religious obligation for an Indian woman. From the religious point of view, marriage is the only Sanskara prescribed for the woman. Only by marriage she is supposed to attain the ultimate aim of life *i.e.* Moksha. "There is a story in Mahabharat, of a lady who remained single because she could not find her equal to marry ; she then devoted her life to the practice of hard penance till old age with a view of obtaining Moksha. But the sage Narada rebuked her for remaining unmarried ; he told her that it was impossible for her to gain the Ultimate Bliss as long as she was not sanctified (sanskarita) by marriage rites."[3a] This being the attitude of the society, towards marriage, married women are respected. The separated, widows and unmarried women are looked down upon and so become vulnerable to the harassment.

From the preceding table, it is clear that the percentage of harassment among separated women is the highest. This phenomenon can be understood only in the context of the ideal of Pativrata as cherished in Indian society, "The ideal of Pativrata *i.e.* being devoted to the husband alone, popularized by the Puranic writers, not merely implied fidelity to the husband but made service to the husband, the only duty of the wife and her main purpose in life.......Her only concern in life was to see that all services needed by her husband were properly performed by her, the satisfaction of her husband being her sole joy in life. Instances are recorded in Puranic literature where a husband demanded that his wife should take him to the house of a prostitute on her shoulder and the wife willingly did it to prove that she was a Sati. As the husband was the centre of all her activities and interests in life, there was no question of raising a word against him even when he was found to be ill-tempered, vicious, deseased or a drunkard."[4] This shows that according to the Indian tradition, the married woman should always be loyal to her husband and her purpose of life is to serve her husband. This tradition persists even now, "In spite of social change Pativrata continues to be the dominant attitude of women towards marriage in large sections of Hindu Society."[5] So, those women who are deserted or separated from husband are thought to be behaving against the sanctions of the society. They lose sympathy of the people. The following remarks bear testimony to this, "Widows are a difficult problem but at least they have the sympathy of society as divorced woman could not, we all feel that we must help widows."[6]

"Without exception the informants expressed their great distaste for the divorce custom of the United States."[7] Mrs. Hate too, hints at the same attitude of the society towards deserted women. She says, "As she has been found from my inquiry, she leaves her husband only under greatest provocation. For she fully knows how society disdains women who forsake or, are forsaken by their husbands."[8]

Faithfulness in marriage is expected in Indian society, especially from woman. Double standard of morality exists for wife and husband. A wife is always expected to be loyal to her husband. By social and religious rituals, the ideal of Pativrata is firmly entrenched into the mind of woman from her very childhood. Husband is not simply a biological mate for her. He is God, and protector for her. So if a woman divorces her husband or is deserted by her husband, she is looked down upon by the people. Divorce is not socially much approved. Even among the lower strata of the society, women, who live alone separated from their husbands are condemned to lower status than those of married women who are loyal to her husband only.

There is a stigma attached to the divorce itself. A woman who is divorced or deserted is always suspected. So, probably that is why divorced or deserted women employees are harassed more than married women employees.

The data also show that widows, to certain extent, are harassed more than married women. The reason of harassment of widows is rightly pointed out by Hate. She says, "The plight of an unmarried girl or a widow seeking remunerative work outside home is much worse than that of a married woman. Her building physique and single life often attract the evil eye of her employer, co-worker or a neighbour. In that case, she runs the risk of falling in the estimation of society."[9]

In Indian society, woman is never thought to be having an independent existence. She is always supposed to be dependant on her close male relatives. So, when a widow lives in a village having separate establishment of her own, is looked down upon.

Kapadia alludes to the plight of a widow in the following way, "Being economically dependant on the members of her husband's family, she was ill treated, abused and sometimes blamed and cursed for any unhappy occurrence in the family. She had to work hard in the house and put up with all kinds of indignities and humiliations from the senior and at times even the junior members of the family. And if this was not sufficiently degrading, she was considered inauspicious. To see her in the morning or to face her while going on a journey or some mission, was regarded a bad omen. Her presence, on any auspicious occasion was considered to forbade calamity and frustration. Consequently, she had to keep herself away or at a distance, even on the occasions of marriage of her own children. Society also made heavy demands on her. She was expected to be chaste. Even if she was seduced by a man outside the family, or more likely in the case of a young and beautiful widow by a member of her family, the man went free and it was the woman who was condemned."[10]

This being the approach of the society towards widow, a widow living an independent life is misunderstood by the people. And so she is harassed.

The data in the present inquiry show that unmarried women are also harassed like widows and separated women. In Indian society it is mainly marriage that confers social status on the woman. Child marriages are in vogue in villages. Unmarried girls past puberty are seldom found in villages. Generally, these unmarried employed women are somewhat of advanced age. In villages unmarried girls from families of higher castes are rarely sent out for employment. So villagers, according to the prevailing norms of the society, interpret the fact of the employment of unmarried adult women as something reflecting on her own prestige and on the prestige of her family. That explains why unmarried women are harassed more.

TABLE 38

Nature of Service of Women Employees and Harassment

Nature of Service	No. of respondents harassed	Total
Nurses	44 (77%)	57
Gramsevikas	33 (57%)	44
Teachers	28 (45%)	62
Total	105	163

(C) Nature of Service and Harassment

An inspection of the above table indicates that Nurses and Gramsevikas are harassed more than teachers.

In Indian society, the profession of nursing does not carry that high status as it should. It is a profession which carries very low prestige. There are very many prejudices about this profession. The following observation of Damle corroborates with this view, "In India there exists in the first place a prejudice against the fact of women working for a living. Firstly it is felt that only those women work for a living who are economically badly off and that their people are not in a position to support them. Secondly, nursing as a career is a taboo since it involves close contact with strangers, leaving aside the concept of pollution."[11] Sengupta (1960) too alludes to the same fact, "In India, however, due to certain social prejudices the nurse has not had the same status as women in other professions."[12] Cormack (1953) too has referred to the same attitude of Indian people towards the nursing profession. She observes, "The attitude of society is much sharper in the case of nurses. Nursing is a below dignity profession".[13] These Nurses are entrusted with the work of making Family Planning propaganda : the work which draws ridicule and negative responses from the people. This has caused a loss of esteem for them in the society. This work is an important part of their duties. Almost all the nurses in the sample complained that it was very difficult for them even to move freely on the road as, obscene remarks are always passed at them by the goondas in the villages.

In Indian society, Sex is a taboo in public life. To talk about Sex openly is regarded as something undesirable. Cormack points out, "Sex is a taboo, just as in urban life....... these things are never talked about."[14] As a part of the official duty Nurses have to explain various things concerned with Family Planning to the people in the village. They have to canvass Family Planning methods even among men. In India, woman is expected to be shy of talking about sexual matters. The modest woman is not supposed to talk openly about Sex. As Nurses are professionally concerned with Family Planning propaganda, they have to talk openly about Sex, so they are regarded as immodest and probably become object of ridicule and harassment.

This peculiar attitude of the people towards nursing profession might be creating trouble for the women who work as Nurses in villages.

Like Nurses, Gramsevikas are also harassed more. Gramsevika has to move freely with the male officers, co-workers, village leaders and the village people. On various occasions, she has to approach the Sirpanch and other village leaders to seek their co-operation for carrying out official programmes. She has to be always in touch with her officers also.

In India, women mixing freely with men outside the family, is not favourably looked at. Those professions in which women have to come in close contact with men, always lose the esteem of the society. Segregation of the sexes is the rule rather than exception, in Indian society. As Dube (1963) points out, "A working wife is economically advantageous ; if she works in a responsible position. She is also a distinct social asset. But her having to mix with others especially with other men is not favourably viewed."[15]

The data in the above table shows that women teachers, as compared with Nurses and Gramsevikas, are less harassed by the villagers. Teaching profession commands respect in Indian society. It is highly eulogised in India, "To achievements in learning, is due the highest honour, according to the Hindu, more even than to achievements in wealth or to elderly relationship or to age."[16] The Mahabharata says, "The father and mother only create body. On the other hand, the life which one acquires from the Guru is divine."[17]

Teacher's profession is old and accepted one. The sanctions of the society for nursing profession and for the profession of Gramsevika are yet to get evolved. So, what Ross (1966) says about new professions is true in this context too. "Some people are probably more strongly conditioned to appropriate sex roles than any others, the above type of conflict would be expected to arise whenever women enter male-typed occupation and to last until both sides have gradually adjusted and women play their roles and are accepted as workers and not as a woman.....,

She will not face this problem when entering on occupation such as teaching, for women have long been accepted in this profession, so both they and the public have made the necessary accommodation."[18] It seems, therefore, that the teachers are less harassed.

From the above discussion, it is clear that the attitude of the society towards the different professions is also responsible for emergence of problems for the working woman.

TABLE 39

Caste of the Women Employee and Harassment

Caste of the woman employee	No. of respondents harassed	Total
Brahmin	35 (64.4%)	57
Middle Castes	44 (67.6%)	65
Lower Castes	15 (78%)	19
Other religions	9 (49%)	22
Total	105	163

(D) Caste and Harassment

Caste is a potent factor in Indian society. The above table indicates that caste is a significant variable in the cases of harassment of women employees. From the above data, it is clear, that women employees belonging to the lower castes are harassed more than those belonging to other castes or religions.

Indian society is stratified in the form of caste structure. Castes are arranged in a hierarchical order. Brahmins occupy the highest ritual status and some castes are pushed to the lowest rung of the social ladder. As they occupy the lowest position, they are made to suffer from various kinds of disabilities.

After Independence, constitutionally and legally the people of the scheduled castes and tribes are getting the opportunities to climb up the social ladder. Aspirations for higher status are created in the minds of these people. Now, they want to relieve themselves off from the dark dungeon of the degraded status accorded to them from the time immemorial. This is not favourably received by the caste Hindus. Because, it disturbs the former equilibrium of inter-relationships among themselves and with it and harms the vested interests of upper castes. The following paragraphs bear a testimony of this view. "Although caste was not the sole determinant of leadership, all leaders were of high caste. Were this the end of it, we might find lower castes to be very nearly powerless and uprooted, their rights neglected."[19] "Culture encouraged a conception of Harijans as in some way less human than others. Under such conditions, one might anticipate antagonism between Harijans and others. The scavenger was educated and met the standards of behaviour of the others, but 'the onus of pollution and the stereotypes of the group were too much."[20] The employment of women of the scheduled castes itself is viewed as the struggle of lower castes to get the higher status.

The entire problem of harassment of the lower caste women can be explained in the following way. After Independence, ideologically and legally, aspirations and opportunities are created for these women. But the ideas of purity and pollution about these people are not changed. The attitude of the society towards these castes is not changed. So, structural constraints are there to thwart these aspirations, newly created in them. Other aspects of society are not yet changed so as to absorb the new trends in this respect. So, structural lag is created which has given rise to the problem of harassment of lower castes women in rural areas.

From the data, it is clear that though particularly the lower castes women are harassed more, the total number of harassment of the women employees is not less. Out of 163 women employees, 105 women said that they were harassed by goondas, leaders and others in the village.

In villages a strong sense of unity is always seen. If a person harasses a stranger, people in the village would be reluctant to expose his name. Employed women are strangers to the village. So they easily become the victims of harassment.

We see economic, political and social factors joining hands to give rise to a peculiar kind of strong power structure in the village which is controlled by the people of the dominant caste. It is often found immune to the legal measures meant for eradicating goondaism in society. This power structure seems to be one of the underlying factors of harassment of women employees.

In Panchayati Raj, the officials are only the executives of the policy determined by the elected representatives of the area. Due to democracy and Panchayati Raj in India, elected leaders weild power even over officials in matters of transfers, promotions etc. So, many times officials are pressurized to do the things as desired by the leaders. If women employees complain against the leaders or their satellites in the village to the officers, the officers are not able to take effective cognizance of such complaints. The officers fear possible interference of the leaders later on. So, the woman employee even though harassed, is not able to complain against goondas or leaders. She has no other go but to succumb to the pressure of these people. All these factors contribute to the harassment of these women employees.

Non-Co-operation of the People

"The concept of the community projects is based on the faith that Gram kalyan can be brought by the joint efforts of the services and the people, if they are properly co-ordinated and directed."[21] It is a project of revitalisation of the community. It is called by the prosaic name of community project, but it is Gram kalyan, a festival of Laxmi."[22]

This being the nature of Community Development Programme, people's co-operation in the implementation of it, is vitally needed. But the data in the present inquiry about the response patterns of the villagers to the employed women who are entrusted with the community project activities tell a different story. Most of the women complained that they do not get adequate co-operation from the people. So, the data in the inquiry was cross-tabulated to see the role of different variables in relation to the co-operation of the people. The following is the cross tabulated data.

TABLE 40

Nature of Service of the Employed Woman and the Pattern of Response of the People

Nature of Service	No. of respondents opposed and ridiculed by the People	Total
Nurses	48 (84.2%)	57
Gramsevikas	30 (68.2%)	44
Teachers	22 (35.9%)	62
Total	100	163

TABLE 41

Caste of the Employee and Pattern of the Response of the People

Caste of the Employee	No. of respondents opposed and ridiculed by the people	Total
Brahmin	28 (49.1%)	57
Middle Castes	42 (64.6%)	65
Lower Castes	17 (89.4%)	19
Other religion	13 (59.1%)	22
Total	100	163

TABLE 42
Marital Status of the Woman Employee and the Pattern of Response of the People

Marital status of the employee	No. of respondents opposed and ridiculed by the people	Total
Unmarried	13 (81.2%)	16
Married	56 (51.3%)	109
Widow	16 (72.7%)	22
Separated	15 (93.7%)	16
Total	100	163

The analysis of the above data taken together show that :

(a) Nurses and Gramsevikas are opposed and denied co-operation than the teachers. (Table 40)

(b) Women employees of the lower castes are opposed and ridiculed more than the employees belonging to other castes. (Table 41)

(c) Unmarried, widow, and separated women employees are opposed and ridiculed more than their married counterparts. (Table 42)

These observations need to be discussed at length :

(a) Though generally, there is a feeling of aversion in the minds of people regarding women taking up employment, yet more and more women are getting into the jobs. However, all the professions in which generally women are absorbed are not equally rated by the people. Professions of teacher and doctor are regarded as prestigious while that of nursing is regarded as a degrading one.

Teacher's profession is eulogised as a noble profession in Indian society. In the Indian tradition, transmission of knowledge is regarded as highest kind of gift, one can bestow on the other. The teacher is equated with God. So, teaching profession always commands respect from the people in India.

Another thing to note in this connection is that Indian village is less urbane. But due to impact of various factors impinging on the rural social system since the last century, urban ways are thought to be worth imitating by the villagers. They think that education is the only means by which they would come on par with the urbanites. Thus, education has instrumental or functional value for them. This, is evident from the growing number of educational institutions in the villages. That is why the teachers do not find much difficulty in securing a positive response from the people.

One more point needs to be taken into consideration is that the teachers are connected with children whose socialisation is yet to be completed. While Nurses and Gramsevikas have to deal, professionally with adults whose interiorization of social roles, attitudes, values, and belief patterns is more or less completed. Children are always adaptive to the new ways of thinking and doing. So, it is easier to secure co-operation from them. Naturally, so far as the teachers are concerned, the problem of non-co-operation and ridicule is not severe. The teacher can fulfil her professional obligations in a more comfortable way than the others.

The role of the Nurse or Gramsevika is concerned mainly with bringing about changes in the traditional attitudes and behaviour patterns of the people. They have to persuade the people to accept the modern ways of life based on rational calculations. For adults, it becomes difficult to adopt or adjust to the new ways and discard set patterns of social life. The following illustrations would bring this point in a clear perspective. If a Gramsevika advises a mother in the village to keep her child clean and tidy : bathe him daily and send the child to school in time : she (mother) would be reluctant to accept this advice, because of fear of possible disturbance in her former role system. It would encroach on her time and energy and on her accepted social ways. This unconsciously, threatens her habituated ways of doing the things. So, such change would be resisted. Naturally, people do not render their co-operation to such programmes, on the contrary they ridicule them. Same is the case with the Nurses role. She is required to advise women in the villages to take proper pre-natal and post-natal care of themselves. For generations, a belief is held among women that birth of a child is a natural thing. If God is kind and merciful, everything would go on smoothly. So, they think human efforts are not of much significance in this context. So, the advice of the nurse falls on deaf ears. That is why nurses always complain of non-co-operation from the people. The conventional beliefs are too hard to break. The following paragraph will illustrate this, "Adoption of modern practices in the field of maternity and child care are also governed by some deep-seated beliefs of the people. A woman is not given any milk in the latter part of her pregnancy and for a month or so, following confinement for fear that this will result in a child too big for normal delivery and will cause swelling and pus formation in the mother's fallopian tubes. For several months, a new born baby is not given any water to drink because this is believed to upset the delicate mechanism of the child's body with its 'cold' effect. The effects of the midwives appointed by the project had very limited success in changing the traditional practices of the community because of the strength of conventional beliefs in this area."[23]

(b) We have earlier discussed the role of caste in the matter of harassment of women. Here too, so far as non-co-operation from the people is concerned, the role of the caste is clearly evident from the data given above. The data show that the scheduled castes women employees are opposed and ridiculed more than the women employees of other castes. The reason is that the lower social status is accorded to them since centuries. And now their attempt to raise themselves in social hierarchy is resented by the upper castes. Another thing is that ideas of purity and pollution still persists in villages. People are selective about, from whom to receive instructions and advice etc. These employed women of the scheduled castes are not accepted by them in this context and so they do not give them co-operation. Thus, caste is one of the important determining factor in the acceptance of agents of change. Dube observes "it is generally, agreed by persons working on action teams that the caste of an extension man materially affects his acceptance—both socially and as an agent of change by the villagers."[24]

(c) Marital status of the women employees is also a significant factor in getting co-operation from the people of the villages. The data indicate that unmarried women, widows and separated women are ridiculed more than married women. As discussed earlier, in the context of harassment of these employees, marriage confers social status on women. And naturally, the corollary of this is that widows and separated women do not get the respect from the people. On the contrary they are ridiculed by the people.

In respect of non-co-operation to unmarried women we have to take into consideration the importance of age factor in Indian society, especially in rural community. Indian rural community is comparatively non-competitive and mainly non-industrial. So, status is still mainly ascribed on the basis of age and sex. A belief is always held by many people in villages that age and wisdom go together. Elderly persons are always supposed to be the source of wisdom, knowledge and experience. They are thought to be fit for giving advice, instructions and guidance to the young people. If the contemporaries or the youngsters try to give advice, it is neglected. Sometimes, fun is made of them. Unmarried women are considered to be immature in age and in experience. The following impression of Dube is worth-noting here in this context. He observes, "Age and experience are considered a desirable, often a necessary, attribute of positions of leadership and influence. As a consequence of this norm, measures initiated by the project always need the blessings and support of the more tradition-bound elders. Projects initiated and run by the younger age groups are viewed as temporary developments of minor significance, and are rarely taken seriously by the Community."[25] So, unmarried women do not get co-operation from the villagers.

The role of employed woman, especially the role of Nurse and Gramsevika, is to persuade the people of villages to accept the modern ways. But the modern ways are completely alien to the village people. Sometimes, these ways are diagonally opposite to their traditional values and way of life. So, they try to resist them. But they lack in the abilities to oppose these ways on intellectual level, and so they try to oppose and ridicule the persons who propagate these ideas. Thus, the employed woman in village becomes the victim of this scapegoat mechanism. She is harassed, ridiculed and opposed by the people in the village.

Another reason of non-co-operation from the people might be that, "people who live in villages are bound together by tradition. Tradition breaks down when the village inhabitants are exposed to new influences from foreign cultures. The villager becomes confused. He does not know, what culture to turn to for answers to his problems. The old way does not seem able to provide the answers and the new does not seem trustworthy."[26] Can it be explained in this way that the presence of alien ideas expose the rural people to milieu of tensions for which their past experience provides inadequate preparation ?

Many respondents said that the village factions also contribute their mite in the harassment of women employees.

From the above discussion, it becomes clear that such variables as nature of service of the employee, her caste, her marital status, her age and the nature of her very role are important determinants in exacting or otherwise, the co-operation of the villagers.

Other Difficulties in the Village

Women employees face many other problems in the villages. They are summarised here,

1. A considerable number of respondents said that village life is drab and dreary. Entertainment or recreation facilities are scarcely available. For entertainment, they have to depend upon the nearby towns or cities.

2. That suitable and adequate educational facilities for their children are not available. In addition, many respondents having young children expressed fear that their youngsters would catch improper unhealthy habits from other children of the villages.
3. They often feel insecure in village atmosphere. Many times goondas and drunkards knock at their doors at odd hours to scarce them.
4. Non-availability of suitable housing accommodation was their another difficulty. They rarely get houses having such essential amenities as bathroom, latrine, water supply and electricity. Lack of these amenities also expose them to many kinds of hardships.

A question whether they feel like leaving the present job was included in the schedule and 82 per cent of the employees expressed their desire to quit the service in the village if they could get job in the city.

Questions were also included in the schedule to know whether they have a genuine interest for the welfare of the rural masses, and whether they identify themselves with the rural people. The tables 43 and 44 show that these women do not very much involve in village social activities, neither they have made any worthwhile attempt on their own for the welfare of rural folk. This fact is expressive in its own way. It shows that these women employees show little interest in villagers and have not identified themselves with them.

The data given in table together highlight the marginal interest, these women employees have in the village life. The very fact that such large majority of women employees are inclined to quit them services clearly reveals this phenomenon.

Summary

The problems of employed women in the context of rural community are studied in this chapter.

That women employees are harassed in rural areas is evident in the present inquiry. The study has tried to locate the social factors responsible for their harassment.

TABLE 43

Participation of Women Employees in Social Activities of the Village

Response	No. of women employees	%
Participated	30	18.40
Not participated	133	81.59
Total	163	

TABLE 44

Have you Started any Organization on your Own for the Welfare of the Rural People ?

Response	No. of women employees	%
Yes	28	17.17
No	135	82.82
Total	163	

From the study, it was clear that the family situation of the employee, her marital status, nature of her service and the caste to which she belongs are the significant factors in relation to her harassment. People harass the employed women who live alone in villages. Women employees who are unmarried, divorced or widowed are more vulnerable to harassment. Nurses and Gramsevikas too, are harassed more than teachers. Caste is also a significant factor.

The peculiar kind of power structure arisen in Maharashtra after Independence, especially after Panchayati Raj, is also a factor playing its role in relation to the molestation of women employees in villages. It is clear from the present study.

The present inquiry has also brought forth the factors responsible for non-co-operation from the villagers. In the context of the developmental activities it, was evident that caste of the woman employee, the nature of her service, her marital status, age etc. are significant variables in getting the co-operation of the villagers. People co-operate with the women employees who are teachers, who belong to higher castes, who are married and who are mature in age and experience.

The role of these women is to provide a kind of dynamic leadership to a tradition-bound community. As innovators, the women employees are expected to guide the rural masses. Their role is to teach them new ways of life based on the scientific, rational, secular, technological and universalistic values and thus help them to solve the main problems of the rural community. But the study has shown that the acceptance, of change agents largely depends upon existing attitudes and social organization of the community.

The question then arises what are the root causes of the problems of employed womem in rural areas ? Can we say that the rural community is passing through the transitional period in which old ways are obsolete and new ways are not satisfactory ? Has, this vacuum-disorder-anomic condition given rise to the problems of women employees as pointed out by Desai (1969), "The rural change that is generated by the Government measures is tending to sharpen the contradictions among various classes in the rural society and in the context of caste and other institutional background is slowly unleashing tensions, antagonisms and collisions."[9]

Halpern detects a ray of hope in this anomy, which the rural community faces today. He says, "The ultimate in order seems to be the antithesis of life. Out of a striving for order may come creative conflict resulting in a stimulating environment of constant change."[27] We can say that these problems, of employed woman in rural areas are the aspects of revolutionary change of one phase of society to the order. The present trends in Indian rural community can be said to be related with growth and development of rural community.

REFERENCES

1. Saksena Devendra N., "Apathy and Social Change in Traditional Societies", an article in "Conspectus of Indian Society" Rajeshwar Prasad *et al.* (Eds.) Satish Book Enterprise, Agra, 1971, p. 391.
2. Myrdal Alva and Klein Viola, "Women's Two Roles" (Routledge and Kegan Paul Ltd., London, 1956) p. 6.
3. Kapadia K.M., "Marriage and Family in India" (Oxford University, Press, Bombay 1966) pp. 253-54.

3a. Prabhu Pandharinath, "Hindu Social Organisation" (Popular Prakashan, Bombay, 1963) p. 150.

4. Kapadia K.M., "Marriage and Family in India" (Oxford University Press, London, 1966) pp. 169-170.
5. Crenstein Henry, "Gaon", (Princeton University Press, Princeton New Jersey, 1965) p. 19.
6. Cormack, Margaret, "The Hindu Woman" (Bureau of Publications, Teachers College, Columbia University, New York 1953) p. 175.
7. *Ibid.*, p. 176.
8. Hate Chandrakala, "Hindu Woman and Her Future" (New Book Co. Ltd., Bombay 1948), p. 222.
9. *Ibid.*, p. 224.
10. Kapadia K.M., "Marriage and Family in India" (Oxford University Press, Bombay, 1966) pp. 173-74.
11. Damle, Y.B., "Auxiliary Nurse Midwife" An Article Published in the Bulletin of the Deccan College Research Institute Poona, Vol. XIX, Nos. 3 & 4.
12. Sengupta Padmini, "Women Workers of India" (Asia Publishing House Bombay, 1960) p. 258.
13. Cormack, Margaret, "The Hindu Woman" (Bureau of Publications, Teachers College Columbia University, New York 1953) p. 170.
14. *Ibid.*, p. 73.
15. Dube, S.C., "Men and Women's role in India" a Sociological review in the Volume : "Women in New Asia" Barbara E. Ward. (Ed.) (UNESCO, Paris, 1963) p. 195.
16. Pandharinath Prabhu, "Hindu Social Organization" (Popular Prakashan Bombay, 1963) p. 125.
17. *Ibid.*, p. 122.
18. Ross Aileen, "The Hindu Family in Urban Setting" (University of Tonroto Press, Bombay, 1966) p. 200.
19. Orenstein Henry, "Gaon" (Princeton University Press, Princeton, New Jersey, 1965) p. 188.

20. *Ibid.*, p. 156.
21. Rajgopalachari C., "Gram Kalyan" An article in 'Kurukshetra' A Symposium on Community Development in India, (Publication Division, Govt. of India, New Delhi, 1961) p. 7.
22. *Ibid.*, p. 8.
23. Dube, S.C., "India's Changing Villages" (Routledge and Kegan Paul Ltd., London, 1960) p. 138.
24. *Ibid.*, p. 139.
25. Narmadeshwar Prasad, "The Cultural Context of technological change and the change agents" An article in "Conspectus of Indian Society," Rajeshwar Prasad *et.al.* (Ed.), (Satish Book Enterprise, Agra, 1971) p. 319.
26. Desai A.R. (Ed.), "Rural Sociology in India" (Popular Prakashan, Bombay, 1969) p. 776.
27. Halpern Joel M., "The Changing Village Community" (Prentice-Hall of India Private Limited, New Delhi, 1969) p. 132.

CHAPTER SIX

SUMMARY AND CONCLUSIONS

THE PROBLEMS of employed woman in rural areas were traced, analysed and discussed in the preceding chapters. Though all of her problems are worthy of investigation, the present study has isolated some of them and examined them from a sociological perspective. The problems relating to her family situation, employment and the rural community are mainly studied in the present work.

It has become evident from the earlier analysis that the employed woman in rural areas suffers from the problems of various kinds arising out of her familial, professional and rural situations. These problems are analysed to bring forth the sociological factors responsible for the same.

Problems in the family of the employed woman are examined to see whether social change conducive to her work-role outside has occurred in the family or not. The role of an employee is one more addition to the former role-complex of house-wife. The employment of woman disturbs the delicate balance of her previous role system. It was noticed in the present analysis that the social change which should have taken place in the family to restore the lost balance is conspicuous by its absence. The kitchen is not at all modernized as to save time and labour of the employed woman. There is no significant attitudinal change in her husband, relatives and the villagers so as to accommodate her as a working woman playing dual roles. The result is that the Indian working woman, unlike the modern western employed woman, has to bear the entire domestic work-load along with the sole responsibility of caring her young ones.

This situation exposes the employed woman to the conflicting role loyalties with the result that the complete fulfilment of both the roles is realistically impossible. And here lies the genesis of her problems in the family. The study has noted down, an intense role-conflict in majority of the cases of these employed women. Apparently the social situation has not become ripe enough to give her concessions in the traditional role expectations about her as house-wife and mother and relieve her for her outside role.

Along with the familial problems, the occupational problems are also studied in this work. Exposure to a completely alien role, incapacities inherent in her personality to handle the occupational role, derogatory, and non-sympathetic treatment accorded to her by the officers, absence of promotions, unfair deals in transfer matters etc. are some of her problems in the occupational field. These problems owe their origin to differential factors.

One reason of her occupational problem is that a change in one aspect of the social system is not followed by corresponding changes in other aspects of the same. The employment of woman is itself a case of social change. But this change has not been followed by changes in other constituents of the social system, such as belief patterns, attitude towards sex, social values etc. These other important constituents of the social system have remained more or less unchanged, *e.g.* women continue to be regarded as inferior to men, in India. So, women are regarded as less reliable workers and are treated accordingly. Men attach significance to the sex-role of woman. Woman, as having an independent personality is never thought of, hence the emergence of her occupational problems.

Another factor responsible for her problems in the occupational field is a clash of two group-values. For generations together, Indian woman is socialised for her primary group relationships only. Now, without adequate formal as well as informal training, she is exposed to impersonal, utilitarian, bureaucratic world of secondary group. So, she faces the problems of adjustment in her new field. Dissatisfaction with the job, inadequacy in handling official procedures, insecurity etc. are the problems in the occupational sphere, emerging due to this clash of values.

Absence of social change in the allied fields, related with the employment of woman, clash of primary and secondary group values and enlargement of status-set demanding conflicting loyalties are the reasons giving rise to the occupational problems of the employed woman in rural areas.

The problems arising out of rural situation are also studied in the present work. Since ages, Indian villages have retained their traditional form. It is in such villages that, women employees are sent to do a pioneering job of introducing innovations based on the scientific outlook. This disturbs the established pattern of life of village people. As Dr. S.C. Dube has pointed out, "When it comes down to the established social practices neither appeals on scientific grounds nor logic can easily persuade the village people to give up their traditional life ways."[1] The innovations disturb the established pattern of life, hence the emergence of her problems.

In the context of rural environment, the main problems from which the employed woman suffers are harassment from the villagers and non-co-operation from them. The study has tried to analyse the factors rerponsible for these problems. It was revealed in the study that different social variables have bearing on these problems. The caste of the employee, nature of employment, family situation, age and marital status of the employee are the significant factors in the context of harassment and non-co-operation from the villagers. Women employees of lower castes suffer from harassment and non-co-operation more than their counterparts of the higher castes. Women teachers are better treated by the villagers than the Nurses and Gramsevikas. The employee of mature age, married and staying with her responsible family members seems to be well-adjusted in village.

The study has noted that the woman employees suffer from various other problems which arise out of rural environment. Lack of facilities of entertainment, scarcity of proper accommodation, lack of educational facilities for children, feeling of insecurity etc. are some of the problems cited by the women employees.

The overall nature of the occupational role of these women employees is of an innovator. Their role is to initiate and assist the process of modernization, in the form of developmental activities sponsored for the rural people. The study has revealed that the acceptance of these woman employees as agents of change by the rural folk depends upon various factors.

This study reiterates the sociological principle that the social system is an integrated whole, so any aspect of it should be analysed in the context of the total social system. So, the problems of employed women cannot be considered as isolated one, but needs to be viewed from the wholistic perspective.

Indian rural community is still tradition-oriented and technologically underdeveloped. The developmental activities sponsored in rural community are the deliberate attempts made by the State for modernizing rural community. The overall nature of the problems of employed woman in rural areas seems to be an aspect of repercussions of modernization of a traditional society.

Modernization tries to bring about continual change in various aspects of society. So, it causes disorganization and dislocation of the organised groups. This results into the emergence of social problems. S.N. Eisenstadt has rightly elaborated this aspect of modernization in the following words, "The very fact, that modernization entails continual changes in all major spheres of a society means of necessity that it involves processes of disorganisation and dislocation, with the continual development of social problems, cleavages and conflicts between various groups and movements of protest, resistance to change. Disorganisation and dislocation thus constitute a basic part of modernization, and every modern and modernizing society has to cope with them."[2]

That modernization, in its wake inevitably creates problems in the modernizing society is succinctly brought out once again by Eisenstadt. He says, "The assurance of a fixed given position which spilled over most of an individual's institutional roles was being continually undermined. It was undermined not only by personal or family fortunes or misfortunes but by the very nature of the system of social organization, by the continual changes and structural differentiation. Hence, although these developments usually opened up new perspectives of advancement and change of status, status necessarily became also a focus of insecurity, awareness and political conflict."[3]

Can we say that the Indian society today, is passing through the turmoils created due to the clash between traditionality and pressure of modernization ? The traditional ascriptive criteria of status based on caste, family, age and sex are getting the challenges from the non-ascriptive, achieved positions, now. Naturally, the vested interest groups based on ascriptive statuses are disturbed. These interest groups are protesting and resisting the change.

The following discussion concerning the Indian situation, will illustrate, how non-ascriptive achieved positions are getting the challenges from traditional groups based on ascriptive statuses.

The higher castes are resenting the encroachment of scheduled castes people upon various fields of social life hitherto denied to them. Likewise, the concept of independent, free earning woman is something new to Indian culture. Hitherto, the general concept of Indian womanhood was that she should be shy, meek, submissive, dependant and confine herself to the four walls of her house. Employed women in villages throw a challenge to these cherished ideas of Indian womanhood. And so, they become victims of harassment. Similarly age is always revered in India. In joint-family, in caste panchayat and in village panchayat, it is the maturity in age that always commands respect. That is why woman employees of younger age are seldom heeded to in villages. Indian society is dominated by men. In India, woman exists for the sake of her husband and her son. She is not expected to have any independent existence of her own but employment brings to her independence in various ways. Thus, employment of woman poses a social threat to these cherished values of society, hence the emergence of her problems.

It can be argued that the problems of employed women in rural areas should not be studied as peculiar problems but should be viewed in the broader context of modernization of traditional society. So, I put forth here certain general observation about modernization of traditional Indian society.

Modernization, requires certain flexibility within the broader social structure. S.N. Eisenstadt points out, "The continuous absorption of change necessarily entails the development of social processes which tend on the one hand to break up any fixed freezing ascriptive arrangements of groups and power structure, while on the other hand they facilitate the continuous restructuring of the distribution of power, wealth and prestige and the re-arrangement of different social groups and roles within common institutional frameworks."[4]

The crucial question is whether Indian society at present, is flexible enough to absorb modernization. If it is not so, what are the factors of persistence of traditional social system ? Once, these factors are located, the hindrances to modernization could be possible to be removed. Then, it would be easier to find solutions for the problems of employed woman. Dr. Cohen points out the following five factors of persistence of the social system in general.[5] Let us test the validity of these factors of persistence in Indian context in the light of his propositions.

(1) "Social systems or structures persist for a number of reasons. The first and most obvious is that infants become social by identifying with their elders and by learning norms, values and beliefs from them...But since all men need some stable points of reference, some anchor in the past, it is probably true, as Comte said, that they are in some respects and to some extent, conservative."

Only after the Independence, the pace of deliberate modernization is accelerated in Indian village. So, most of the people of recent generations are socialised with the traditional norms, values, beliefs etc. of the society. So, they are conservative in nature. This conservatism creates hurdles in the path of modernization.

(2) "The second reason for social persistence is that norms prescribe what is typical or predictable and that some men, at least, develop a vested interest in this."

In Indian society people belonging to higher castes, people of mature age and men compared to women have developed a vested interest in the established pattern of society. The problems of employed women are created because in many respects the employment of woman, poses a challenge to the vested interest groups in the traditional society.

(3) "The third reason for social persistence is the force of legitimacy...for it is not simply that men prefer the familiar but that they come to accept it as right, and that they must be highly motivated to oppose it."

In Indian society, the traditional norms, values and behaviour patterns have not only social sanctions but religious sanctions too, *e.g.* caste-rules have the sanction of religious scriptures. So, because of force of double legitimacy to the existing social norms, modernization is opposed. That explains why employed women do not get positive response.

(4) "The fourth reason, for persistence is the 'deadweight effect' of integration between institutions, beliefs etc. Any pressure for change in one or of social life may be resisted because of the 'reinforcement effect' of different parts of social systems on one another."

In Indian society, the caste, the joint family and the village panchayat are the main traditional institutions which enforce each other. So, modernization is resisted.

(5) "The final and some would say the most important reason for social persistence is vested interest ; there are always some groups in a society who either have an interest in preserving a particular system or who prefer the status quo to the uncertainties of particular type of change."

Indian rural society is made to change through deliberately introduced change in the form of developmental programme. People may be preferring the status quo to the unfamiliar change, because of element of uncertainty involved in it.

These are some of the factors responsible for the persistence of traditional Indian social structure. These factors resist modernization. The problems of the employed woman in rural areas should be viewed in the context of modernization. Once the factors of persistence in the traditional society are located, the hindrances to modernization could be removed. The problems of employed woman are created due to the inroads of modernity on traditional social structure which is not yet ready to welcome it.

Points To Ponder

This study, of the particular problems of those employed women has revealed that the woman employee is exposed to the conflicting sets of expectations to both the roles in such a way that complete fulfilment of both the roles is realistically impossible. In either case, deviance from the expected role is inevitable. Deviance in either case on the part of woman worker would not be favourable for carrying out developmental schemes meant for millions of rural people.

If the woman deviates from her expected role in the family, more problems would be created in the family, which in turn would affect her role performance as an employee adversely. If the woman worker is unable to adhere to the minimum expectations of her work-role that too, would prove detrimental to the developmental programmes. But we cannot dismiss the schemes envisaged for the welfare of the millions, merely because problems are created. Dr. Dube has a word of praise for the developmental schemes in the following way :

"So much needs to be done in village India to-day that any organised effort like this is bound to earn the praise of those who are interested in human welfare."[6] T.S. Avinashlingam too, expresses the same view, "The community development movement and the Panchayati Raj organization continue to be the only means of rural development in our country, involving nearby 80 per cent of our population. Therefore, this movement cannot be lightly dismissed as a failure......Wisdom consists in spotting the defects and removing them so that the process of development continues unhindered. Therefore we should consider ways and means of improving it."[7]

These woman workers in villages are appointed for the improvement of the rural women folk. Due to various problems engulfing them, these women workers are unable to play their occupational role properly. So, unless their problems are solved, they would not be able to play their work-role effectively. So, let us consider the measures for eradicating the difficulties of employed woman in rural areas, so that it would be possible for her to devote herself single mindedly to her professional role.

It is a common observation that the higher officials and persons occupying important positions in the Government services, are provided with many amenities to maintain their prestige in society. They are provided with fabulously furnished rent-free houses, paraphernalia of servants at their back and call and many other allowances. Why not these employed women in rural areas receive a small part of the charity of the democratic government wedded to the idea of socialism? These women too, play an important role in bringing about social change in rural community.

Much of the time and energy of the employed woman in rural areas is wasted in doing monotonous household work. To lighten her domestic burden, the Government should give subsidies to employed woman to buy labour saving gadgets such as pressure cooker, gas ovens, electric-mixer, small refrigerators and other kitchen kits. This would serve the double purpose ; one, reducing the hours of work in the kitchen and secondly raising up the social prestige of these women, as these gadgets are regarded as the expressive symbols of prestige in our society.

In the present study it was noticed that considerable number of respondents have very young children. The employed mothers having young children should be given a special treatment by the Government. Extra allowances for childrens' food and for baby, sisters should be given to them. In addition to this, a sympathetic consideration should be offered in the transfer matters and in granting leaves of absence. Employed mothers having children above the age of six, should be given some monetary help for the education of their wards, so that their education would not suffer on account of the employment of their mothers. Mothers, who would be transferred to remote villages would be able to make some arrangement in towns or cities for the education of their children with this money. Our welfare State should not consider, bringing up of children as the sole responsibility of the parents. It should help those who urgently need it.

Five-days-week or reducing the daily hours of work by 2 hours, at least a day, for the women workers is worth trying out, as we are interested in the results and not in the hours, of work. We should always keep in mind that employed woman carries over the double burden of home and work. Reduced hours of professional work would recoup her energy and in the long term would be able to do justice to her work-role outside.

If the domestic problems are solved to the satisfaction of the employed woman, it is possible that she would be free from intense role-conflict which was evidenced in the present study.

As we noted earlier, the problems in the occupational sphere have arisen by the virtue of the fact that these women have very low educational qualifications, and they are not adequately oriented to their new role. Though, some vocational training is given to them. But along with it, some arrangement for the training in the official procedures and formalities for them is also needed. Women with higher educational qualifications are not attracted to these professions. If above mentioned amenities are offered to these jobs, there is every likelihood that women with higher qualifications would be attracted to these posts.

From the study, it was noted that these women are often transferred to distant places. So, many problems such as no help from relatives, insecurity, wastage of money in travelling etc. have arisen. If the women are transferred to the places nearer to, or within their home-districts, many of these problems would be eliminated. While thinking of work-role, one has to take into consideration the contentment of the worker. If the worker is satisfied with his work and if free from personal worries, he would devote whole-heartedly to his work. As Myrdal and Klein, stresses the same view point (1956) when they observes, "Among those concerned with the welfare of the population, the view has increasingly gained ground that not only in the homes, but also in the organization of work and leisure pursuits, more account should be taken of the fact that working men and women are not isolated individuals but members of families. The problem is how best to strike a balance between the economic interests of increased productivity and the social aim of contentment among the workers and their families alike."[8]

From the data collected in the present study it was revealed that very few possibilities of promotions exist in their jobs. Promotions are the mechanisms to elicit expected role performance in the occupational field. So, some more provisions for promotions are needed.

The study has brought to light that there are no concerted efforts on the part of these women, to get their problems solved. United efforts on the part of these women would help them to better their conditions.

Some of the problems of employed women owe their origin to the tendency of persistence of traditional social structure in rural areas. As we are aware that change in social attitude, belief patterns, values etc. is a slow process which cannot be brought about by mere administrative measures. As Alva Myrdal and Viola Klein say, "Social Progress always proceeds at an unequal pace in different fields of human activities. It has, as a rule, followed roughly the pattern, namely that new scientific inventions lead to technical advances within their turn, are followed by social adjustments and reorganization; changes in general attitudes and opinions usually bring up the rear."[9] So, slow hammering in the form of propaganda regarding different aspects of modernization is the need of the time.

"One of the chief characteristics of modern India is the rapid development of community projects in rural areas. If the plans are implemented according to the schedule, sleeping villages would awaken into activity, defeating ignorance, poverty, superstitions and reactionary tradition. Especially will women and children benefit from the many plans and projects, so carefully drawn up for them."[10]

The employment of woman would have a far-reaching influence in our society. If she fails in playing her occupational role it would only damage the status of employed woman in society. If she triumphs over the difficulties, the lives of rural women would take on a new significance.

On a theoretical plane, some comprehensive study needs to be undertaken of the deep-seated reasons of the choice of these jobs by the women workers in rural areas. The effects of the employment on her other important familial relations, such as marital, parental and kinship and in turn their effects on her employment are worthy of studying. This would serve a double purpose. It would throw more light on success or failure of the development programmes and it would reveal the hidden factors related to the employment of woman in general.

The impression gathered about the developmental programme for rural women folk is that it is not satisfactory. To make the programme a success, a study of cultural factors such as belief patterns, habits, world-views, social values, attitudes and class structure of rural women needs to be undertaken by the social scientists.

REFERENCES

1. Dube, S.C., "India's Changing Villages." (Routledge and Kegan Paul Ltd., London, 1960) p. 134.
2. S.N. Eisenstadt, "Modernization : Protest and Change" (Prentice Hall of India Pvt. Ltd., New Delhi, 1969) p. 20.
3. *Ibid.*, p. 11.
4. *Ibid.*, p. 151.
5. Cohen, P.S., "Modern Social Theory" (Heinemann Educational Book Ltd., London. 1968) pp. 157-159.
6. Dube, S.C., "India's Changing Villages" (Routledge and Kegan Paul Ltd., London, 1960) p. 147.
7. Avinashlingam, T.S., "Retrospect and Prospect" (An article in 'Community and Panchayati Raj Digest' issue, dated 2nd Oct., 1970.) p. 82.

8. Alva Myrdal and Viola Klein, "Women's Two Roles" (Routledge and Kegan Paul Ltd., London, 1956) p. 195.
9. *Ibid.*, p. 197.
10. Sengupta, Padmini, "Women Workers of India" (Asia Publishing House, Bombay, 1960) p. 216.

Appendix A

CASES OF MOLESTATION OF WOMAN EMPLOYEES AS REPORTED IN THE NEWSPAPERS

(1) Miss S.K. was working as a Gramsevika at Bhivapur in Vidarbha region of Maharashtra. She was 28 and was from a middle class family. One day she was found burnt to death in her official quarter at Bhivapur in broad day-light. It was told that the woman was harassed by her officer.

The letter written by Miss S.K. prior to her death, to the Executive Officer of Zilla Parishad throws some light on the incident. She wrote in her letter, "Yesterday evening at 7 p.m., a small cycle rikshaw was brought to my residence by the officer. Already there were four persons sitting in it. The officer told me to accompany them on tour. Often these things are repeated. I fear my modesty and life are not safe here because of this officer. So I entrust you to transfer me immediately and relieve me from the clutches of this officer."

Afterwards the case was tried in the Court.

(2) Miss K.P. was working as an auxiliary nurse-midwife at Aurad Shahajani in Osmanabad District of Maharashtra. She died because of unsuccessful abortion. It was said that her officer was responsible for her pregnancy. He disowned it and the tragedy took place.

(3) Miss K.V. was working as a Gramsevika in one of the villages of Thana District of Maharashtra. One day, she was found murdered on road. One Adivasi was alleged of her

murder. It was rumoured that some influential leaders were involved in this incident. The case was tried in the Court and was discussed on the floor of the Maharashtra Assembly.

(4) Mrs. G., an auxiliary nurse-midwife, was posted in a village of Nasik district of Maharashtra. One day, she was found dead in hanged condition in her very small room. That whether it was a case of suicide or of a murder could not be ascertained. Mystery surrounds the whole incident. It was reported that Mrs. G. sometime back, tried for her transfer, because she was harassed by the villagers. She was transferred and so she was about to leave the place. It was rumoured that some persons in the village borrowed money from her and as she was transferred, she asked for repayment and it resulted into her death.

(5) Miss M.G. was working as a Family-Planning-field-worker in a village. The Sirpanch of the Village (Head of the Village Council) belonging to the ruling party, tried to molest her.

The case is that one day she was sleeping in the courtyard of her house. The Sirpanch came to her and tried to rape her. He threatened her that nobody in the village would dare to come to her rescue. So better she submit to his desire.

(6) Miss I.S. was working as a Family-Planning-worker at Patoda centre of Osmanabad district of Maharashtra.

One day, at night at about 11.30 p.m., a jeep belonging to the Panchayat Samiti was sent to her, on the pretext that she was called by the officer. She was taken to the lonely place in the jeep. There, the driver and four other persons tried to rape her. But the woman, anyhow managed to rescue herself. This incident was discussed publicly and also on the floor of Maharashtra Assembly.

(7) Mrs. S.S. was working as teacher in a village in Bhir district. She complained to the police on 29th Dec., 1971 that she was molested on a road in the broad daylight by the younger brother of village Sirpanch. She added that, prior to the incident, the village Sirpanch paid a visit to her school and told her that like the lady teacher who satisfied the desire of Sirpanch in the Marathi film "Ek Gaon Bara Bhangadi"

she should also fulfil his wish. The molestation followed her denial.

(8) "The recent frightful and shocking incident at Koregaon, a village in the Walwa Taluka of Sangli district of Maharashtra reveals how dangerous it is for young girls and women to stay all alone in villages to carry out their duties.

The story goes, Miss N.R.N. was appointed Nurse at the Family Planning Centre, Koregaon. She went for shopping to Bagni, a nearby village, in a touring car belonging to a person in the village. She was accompanied by her female attendant. On their way back home in the touring car, a group of persons with axes and lathis in their hands, stopped the car. It was 9.30 p.m. and there was complete darkness around. The miscreants threatened the driver and asked him to put off the lights. Then with the help of a torch, they found out where the young Nurse was sitting, and dragged her out of the car and led her to a nearby jowar farm.

The woman employee struggled hard to free herself from their clutches. By this time, she was crying out loudly for help but none of onlookers dared to come to her rescue because of the fear of the goondas. To stop her loud cries, one of the miscreants took off his cap and stuffed it into her mouth. All the while she entreated them to have mercy on her, treat her as their daughter, sister and save her honour, but none paid any heed to her cries. The goondas are believed to have torn her clothes completely in a bid to molest her. They threatened the woman and other persons in the car with the words "Keep quiet ; otherwise be prepared for the consequences."

BIBLIOGRAPHY

Altekar, A.S., "The Position of Women in Hindu Civilization" (Motilal Banarsidas, Delhi, Patna, Varanasi 1956).

Appadorai, A. (Ed.), "Status of Women in South Asia" (Orient Longmans Ltd., Delhi, 1954).

Ali-Beg, Tara, "Women of India" (Publication Division, Ministry of Information and Broadcasting, Government of India, Delhi, 1958).

Avinashlingam, T.S., "Retrospect and Prospect" (Article in Community and Panchayati Raj Digest" 2, October 1970).

Bajpai, S.R., "Methods of Social Survey and Research" (Kitab Ghar, Kanpur, 1966).

Burchinal Lee, G., "Factors Related to Employment of Wives in a Rural Iowa County" (Agricultural and Home Economics Experimental Station, Iowa State, University of Science and Technology, Research Bulletin, October 1962).

Bertrand, "Rural Sociology" (McGraw Hill Book, Inc. 1958)

Beverly Benner Cassara (Ed.), "American Woman, the Changing Image" (Beacon Press, Boston, 1962).

Beals Alan R., "Gopalpur" (Holt, Rinehart and Winston, New York, 1962).

Bhatnagar, N.K., "Status of Women and Family Planning in India" (The Journal of Family Welfare Vol., XVIII No. 3, March 1972).

Bank, Olive, "Women's Two Roles" (A Book review), (British Journal of Sociology, Vol. VIII, No. 1, March 1957) p. 75.

Cormack, Margaret, "The Hindu Woman" (Bureau of Publications, Teachers College Columbia University, New York, 1953).

Chauhan, Brij-Raj, "A Rajasthan Village" (VIR Publishing House, New Delhi-5, 1967).

Cohen, P.S., "Modern Social Theory" (Heinemann Educational Book Ltd., London, 1968).

Cohen, A.K., "Deviance and Control." (Prentice-Hall of India Pvt. Ltd., New Delhi, 1970).

Devis, Kingsley, "Human Society" (The Macmillan Company, New York, 1967).

Damle, Y.B., "Auxiliary Nurse Midwife." (Article in the Bulletin of the Deccan College Research Institute, Poona, Vol. XIV, Nos. 3 and 4).

Dahlstrom, Edmund (*Ed.*), "The Changing Roles of Men and Women" (Gerald Duckworth and Co. Ltd., London, 1967).

Dube, S.C., "India's Changing Villages" (Routledge and Kegan Paul Ltd., London, 1960).

Dube, S.C., "Indian Village" (Routledge and Kegan Paul Ltd., London, 1959).

Department of Scientific and Industrial Research, London, "Woman, Wife and Worker" (Her Majesty's Stationary Office, Booklet 1960).

Desai, A.R., "Rural India in Transition" (Popular Book Depot, Bombay, June 1961).

Desai, A.R. (*Ed.*), "Rural Sociology in India" (Popular Prakashan, Bombay, 1969).

Eisenstadt, S.N., "Modernization, Protest and Change" (Prentice-Hall of India Private Ltd., New Delhi, 1969).

Gadgil, D.R., "Women in Working Force in India" (Asia Publishing House, Bombay, 1965).

Ghildyal, U.C., "The Ecology of Community Development in India', (Community Development and Panchayati Raj Digest, Oct. 1970).

Goode, W. and Hatt, P., "Methods in Social Research" (McGraw-Hill, 1952).

Gore, M.S. et. al. (Eds.), "Papers in the Sociology of Education in India" (National Council of Educational Research and Training, Bombay, 1967).

Ghurye, G.S., "Caste, Class and Occupation" (Popular Book Depot, Bombay, 1961).

Gupta, Anup, "The Problems of Working Women" (An Article in 'Yojana' Govt. of India Publication, Issue of March 21, 1971).

Govt. of Maharashtra, "Problems Facing Women Employees in Government Service : Report of the Committee" (General Administration Deptt., Govt. of Maharashtra, Bombay, 1972).

Hingane Stree Shikshan Sanstha (Ed.), "Bhartiya Stree".

Hate, C. (Mrs.), "Hindu Woman and Her Future" (New Book Company Ltd., Bombay, 1948).

Hunter, Guy, "Modernizing Peasant Societies" (Oxford University Press, London, 1969)

Hiebert Paul G., "Konduru" (University of Minnesota Press, Minneapolis, 1971).

Hacker Helen, "The Feminine Protests of the Working Wife" (Indian Journal of Social Work, Vol. XXXI No. 4, Jan. 1971. pp. 401-406).

Halpern, J.M., "A Changing Village Community" (Prentice Hall of India Pvt. Ltd., New Delhi, 1969).

Jephcott, Pear et. al., "Married Women Working" (George Allen and Unwin Ltd., London, 1962).

Johnson, Harry, "Sociology" (Allied Publishers Private Limited, Bombay, 1966).

Jeffery Margot, "Married Women in the Higher Grades of the Civil Service and Government Sponsored Research Organizations" (The British Journal of Sociology, Vol. III, No. 1, March 1962, p. 361).

Kapoor (Mrs.) Promilla, "Marriage and the Working Woman in India" (Vikas Publishing House, New Delhi, 1971).

Kapadia, K.M., "Marriage and Family in India" (Oxford University Press, Bombay, 1966).

Karve, Irawati, "The Indian Women in 1975" (Indian Institute of Public Administration, New Delhi, 1966).

"*Kurukshetra*" A symposium on Community Development in India" (The Publication Division, Govt. of India, Delhi, July 1961).

Klein, Viola, "Employed Married Women" (British Journal of Sociology, Vol. XIV, No. 1, pp. 85-86).

Klein, Viola, "Working Wives" (Institute of Personnel Management, London, 1959).

Lewin, D., "Reasons for Women Going Out to Work and Family Relations" (Ref. Sociological Abstract 1970), p. 822.

Ministry of Community Development and Co-operation, Govt. of India, "Gram Sevika" A Pamphlet, July 1960.

Merton, R.K., "Social Theory and Social Structure" (The Free Press Glencoe, Illinois, 1961).

Myrdal Alva & Viola Klein, "Women's Two Roles" (Routledge and Kegan Paul Ltd., London, 1956).

Ministry of Labour and Employment, Govt. of India, "Women in Employment" (Labour Bureau, Govt. of India 1964).

Mancker, R.B., "Lower Pay for Women" A Case of Economic Discrimination (Industrial Relation 10 (3) Oct. 1971, pp. 316-326).

Morries, Brian, "Reflections on Role Analysis" (The British Journal of Sociology, Vol. XXII, No. 4, December 1971, p. 395).

Mackim, Marriott, "Village India" (The University of Chicago Press, Chicago, 1960).

Mehta Rama, "The Western Educated Hindu Woman" (Asia Publishing House, 1970).

Maharashtra Census Office, "Census of India, 1961 District Census Hand Book, Parbhani" (Government of Maharashtra, Bombay, 1965).

Maharani of Baroda H.H. and Mitra M., "The Position of Women in Indian Life" (Longmans, Green and Co., London, 1912).

Parsons, Talcott, "Social System" (Tavistock Publications Ltd., London, 1952).

Prabhu Pandharinath, "Hindu Social Organisation" (Popular Prakashan, Bombay, 1963).

Prasad Rajeshwar, et. al. (Ed.), "Conspectus of Indian Society" (Satish Book Enterprise, Agra, 1971).

Piotrowski, J.C., "The Employment of Married Women and Changing Sex Roles" (Ref. Sociological Abstracts Feb.-April 1970, p. 847).

Ranade, S.N. and P. Ramchandran, "Women and Employment" (Tata Institute of Social Sciences, Bombay, 1970).

Ross Aileen D., "The Hindu Family in its Urban Setting" (University of Toronto Press, Bombay, 1966).

Sen Gupta Padmini, "Women Workers of India" (Asia Publishing House, Bombay, 1960).

Spaulding Charles B., "An Introduction to Industrial Sociology" (D.B. Taraporevala Sons and Co. Private Ltd., Bombay, 1970).

Sinha, Durganand, "Indian Villages in Transition" (Associated Publishing House, Delhi, 1969).

Srinivas, M.N. (Ed.), "India's Villages" (Asia Publishing House, Bombay, 1960).

Smith, S.H., "Managers and Married Women Workers" (The British Journal of Sociology, Vol. XII, No. 1, pp. 12-22).

Stewart, C.W., "Future Trends in Employment of Married Women" (The British Journal of Sociology, Vol. XII, No. 1, pp. 1-11).

Sirsikar, V.M., "The Rural Elite in a Developing Society" (Orient Longmans Ltd., Poona 4, 1970).

Sharp, L.J., "Employment Status of Mothers and Some Aspects of Mental Illness" (American Sociological Review, Vols. 1 to 25, 1936-60).

Turner, R.H., "Some Aspects of Women's Ambition" (American Journal of Sociology, Vol. LXX, No. 3, 1964).

Venkatrayappa, K. N., "Feminine Roles" (Popular Prakashan Bombay, 1966).

Ward, Barbara (Ed.), "Women in New Asia" (UNESCO, Paris, 1963).

Worsley, Peter et. al. (Ed.), "Modern Sociology, Introductory Readings" (Penguin Books Ltd., Harmondsworth, Middlesex, England, 1971).

Worsley, Peter et. al. (Ed.), "Introducing Sociology" (Penguin Books Ltd., Harmondsworth Middlesex, England, 1971).

Zahir Ahmed, "Dusk and Dawn in Village India" (Pall Mall Press Ltd., London, 1965).